Table of Contents

About the Author

With over 20 years' experience in the computer industry, Kevin Wilson has made a career out of technology and showing others how to use it. After earning a master's degree in computer science, software engineering, and multimedia systems, Kevin has held various positions in the IT industry including graphic & web design, programming, building & managing corporate networks, and IT support.

He serves as senior writer and director at Elluminet Press Ltd, he periodically teaches computer science at college, and works as an IT trainer in England while researching for his PhD. His books have become a valuable resource among the students in England, South Africa, Canada, and in the United States.

Kevin's motto is clear: "If you can't explain something simply, then you haven't understood it well enough." To that end, he has created the Exploring Tech Computing series, in which he breaks down complex technological subjects into smaller, easy-to-follow steps that students and ordinary computer users can put into practice.

You can contact Kevin using his email address:

office@elluminetpress.com

About the Author

Acknowledgements

Thanks to all the staff at Luminescent Media & Elluminet Press for their passion, dedication and hard work in the preparation and production of this book.

To all my friends and family for their continued support and encouragement in all my writing projects.

To all my colleagues, students and testers who took the time to test procedures and offer feedback on the book

Finally thanks to you the reader for choosing this book. I hope it helps you gain a better understanding of Python Programming.

Getting Started

The aim of this book is to provide a first course in the use of a methodical and effective approach to the development of computer programs using the Python Programming Language.

Chapters have been deliberately kept short with a learn by doing approach. Along the way, you'll find various video tutorials and demonstrations you can access using the various links throughout the book.

Chapter by chapter, we'll explore the ins and outs of Python with illustrations, worked examples, lab exercises and projects for you to complete yourself. For this purpose, we've included all the source code for this book in the following repository:

`elluminetpress.com/python2`

Have Fun!

What is Python

Python is a high-level programming language created by Guido van Rossum and first released in 1991. The name "Python" was inspired by Guido's love for the British comedy series "Monty Python's Flying Circus".

Python emphasizes code readability and aims to provide a clear and concise syntax, making it easier for programmers to express concepts and ideas in fewer lines of code compared to other programming languages. There is also a comprehensive library that provides a wide range of built in modules and functions for common programming tasks. This philosophy encourages the reuse of existing code and reduces the need for developers to rely heavily on third-party libraries for basic functionalities. Over the years, Python has attracted a large community of developers who contribute to its extensive ecosystem of third-party libraries and frameworks, further expanding its capabilities.

Python is designed to be a versatile language and is widely used in web development, data analysis, artificial intelligence, scientific computing, and automation.

Installing Python

In this section, we'll take a look at how to install the python interpreter and development environment.

Python has multiple versions available, such as Python 2.x and Python 3.x. It is recommended to install the latest stable version, which is Python 3.x. Python 2.x is no longer actively supported, and most new projects and libraries are designed for Python 3.x.

You can install python on Windows, Mac, or linux.

Install on Windows

In our lab, we're using windows workstations, so we'll need to install the Python Development Environment for Windows.

Open your web browser and navigate to the following website:

`www.python.org/downloads/windows`

From the downloads page, select the 'executable installer' of latest stable release.

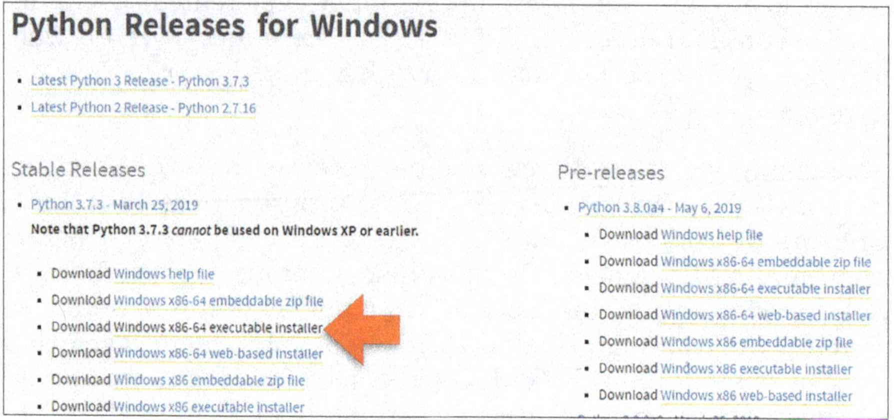

Click 'run' when prompted by your browser. Or click 'python-x.x.x-amd64.exe' if you're using Chrome.

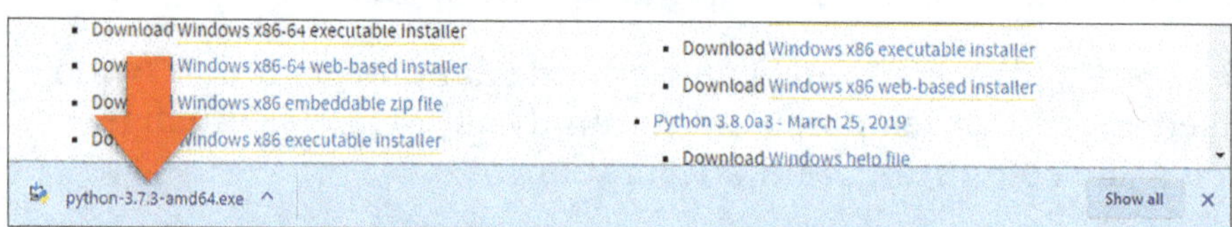

Once the installer starts, make sure 'add python 3.x to path' is selected, then click 'customize installation' to run through the steps to complete the installation.

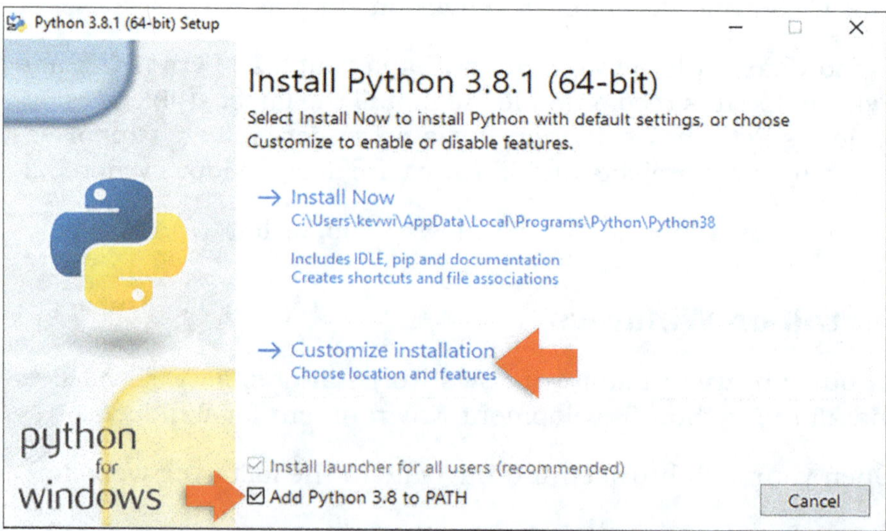

Make sure you select all the tick boxes for all the optional features. Click 'next'.

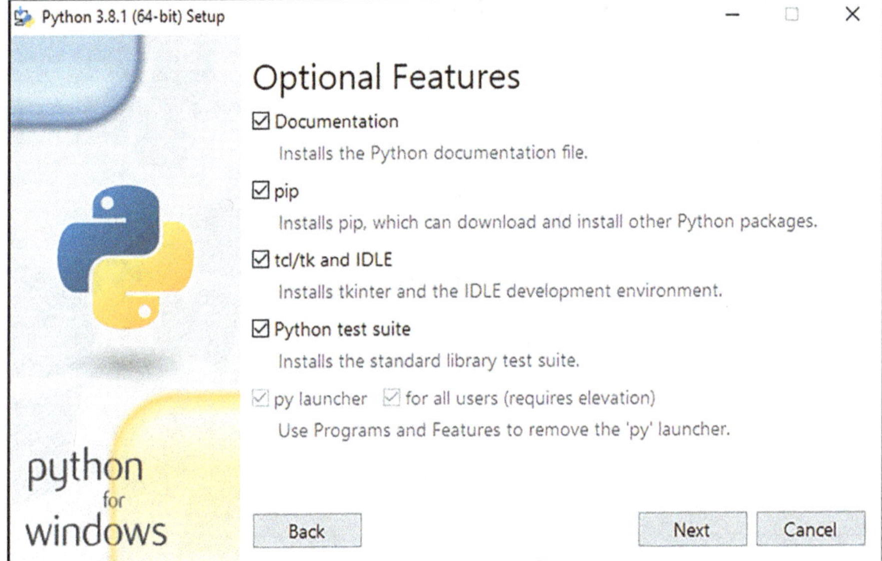

Make sure 'install for all users' is selected at the top of the dialog box. Click 'install' to begin.

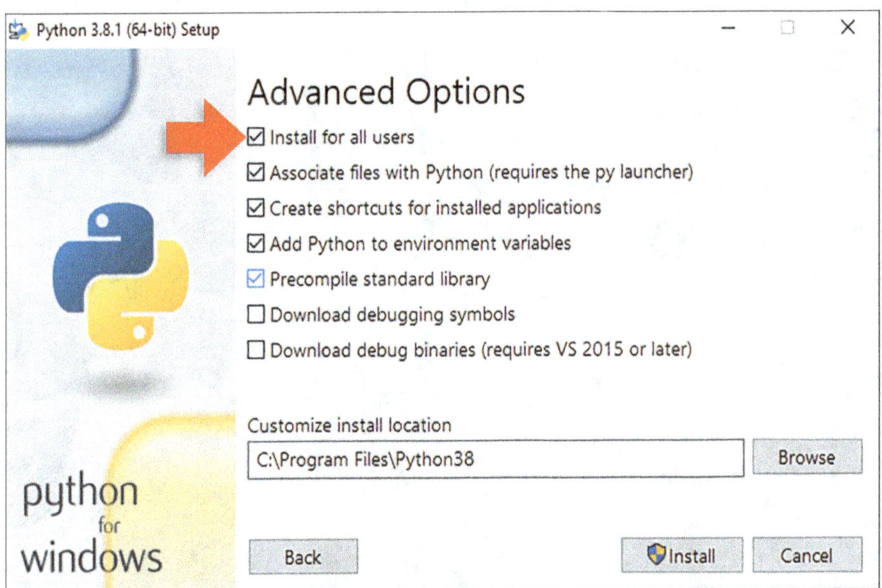

Click 'disable path length limit' to make sure Python runs smoothly on Windows and allow long file names.

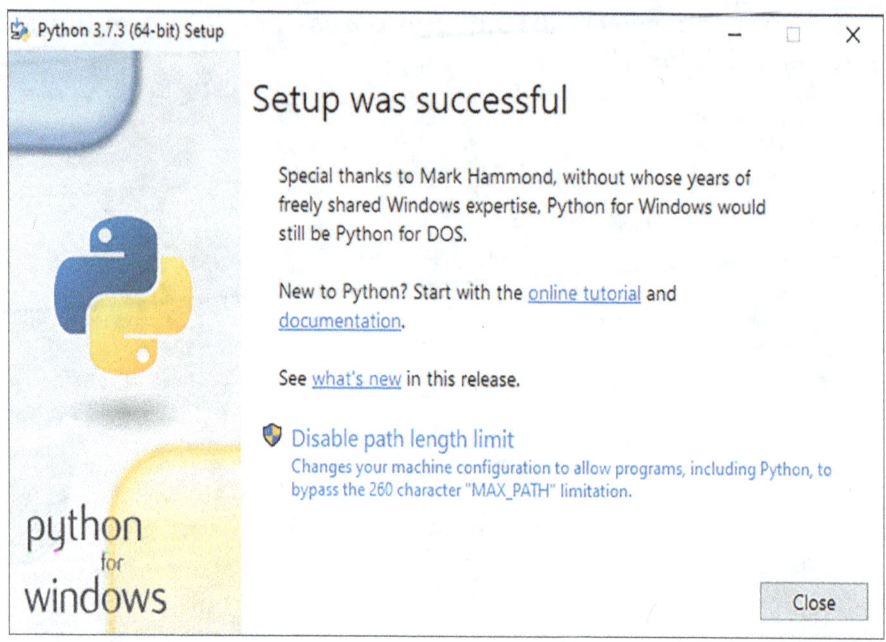

Click 'close' to finish the installation.

You'll find the Python Development Environment (IDLE) and the Python interpreter, in the Python folder on your start menu.

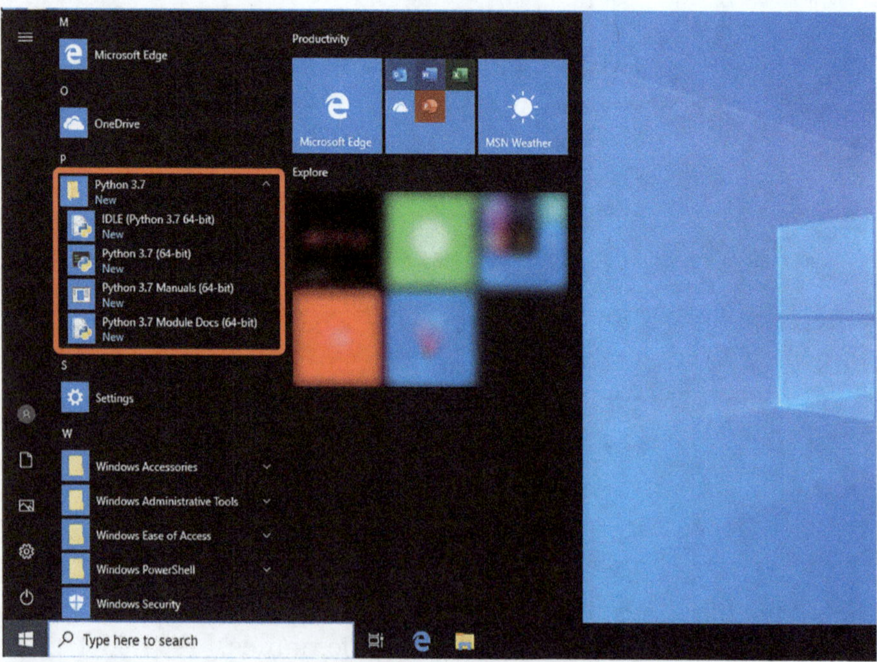

Install on MacOS

To install Python 3 with the Official Installer, open your web browser and navigate to the following website

```
www.python.org/downloads/macos
```

Click download python.

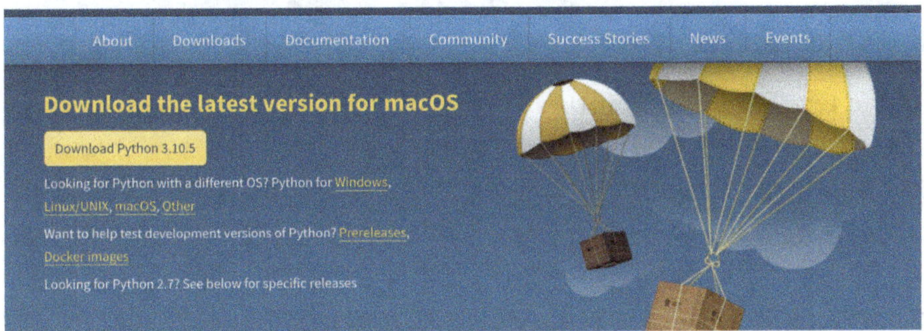

You'll find the package in your downloads folder. Double click on the package to begin the installation

Run through the installation wizard. Click 'continue'.

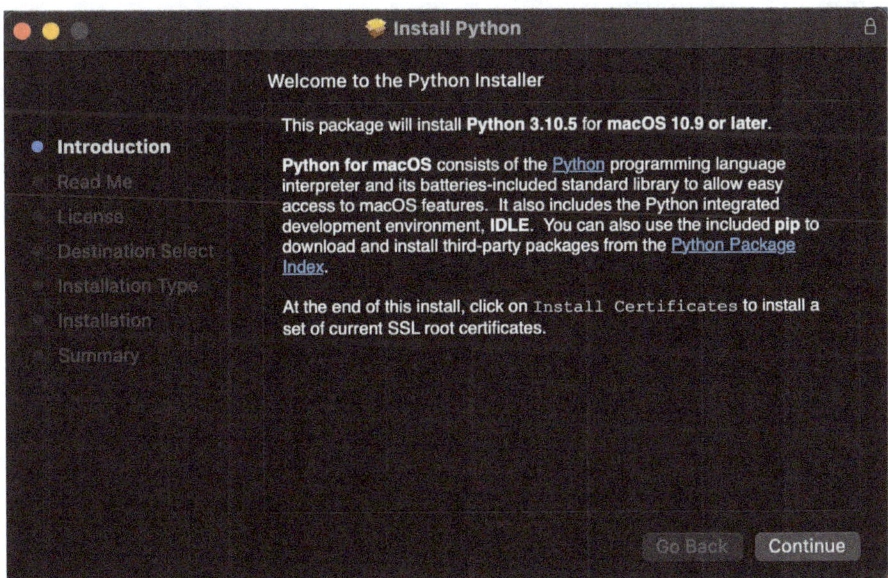

Once the installation is complete, you'll find python in the applications folder in finder, or on the launch pad.

Install on Linux

If you are running a linux distribution such as Ubuntu or have a Raspberry Pi, you can install python using the terminal. You'll find the terminal app in your applications. You can also press Control Alt T on your keyboard.

At the terminal command prompt, type the following commands. Press enter after each line.

```
sudo apt update
```

```
sudo apt upgrade
```

Type the following command to install Python.

```
sudo apt install python3 -y
```

Once the Python is installed, we need to install IDLE, the development environment. To do this, type the following command at the prompt

```
sudo apt-get install idle3 -y
```

Once installed, you'll find IDLE in your applications.

Or you can type the following command at the prompt

```
idle
```

Setting up a Development Environment

A good development environment enhances productivity by providing features such as code editing, debugging, and testing capabilities.

There are several code editors and Integrated Development Environments (IDEs) available for Python programming. Once you have installed the python interpreter as discussed above, you should install a code editor or IDE. What you choose is personal preference and depends on the specific requirements of your project.

Try a few difference ones until you find the one that suits your needs the best.

Code Editor vs IDE

A code editor is a lightweight tool focused primarily on editing code. It provides features such as syntax highlighting, code completion, and basic code formatting. Some popular code editors are Visual Studio Code and Sublime Text.

An IDE is a comprehensive software suite that combines a code editor with additional tools and features specifically designed for software development. In addition to code editing capabilities, IDEs typically provide features like debugging, code refactoring, project management, and version control integration. Examples of popular IDEs include PyCharm, IDLE and Eclipse.

You should also consider an interactive computing environment. This is a software environment that allows you to interactively write and execute code while providing immediate feedback and results. Within this environment you can write code, run it, and see the output in real-time, facilitating an iterative and exploratory approach to programming.

Jupyter Notebook is a popular interactive computing environment that allows you to create and share documents containing live code, visualizations, and explanatory text.

Visual Studio Code (VS Code)

Visual Studio Code is a lightweight and highly customizable code editor developed by Microsoft.

`code.visualstudio.com`

It has excellent Python support with features such as IntelliSense which provides context-aware suggestions for functions, methods, variables, and modules as you type, helping you write code faster and with fewer errors.

VS Code also offers debugging tools and a wide range of extensions that enhance Python development experience.

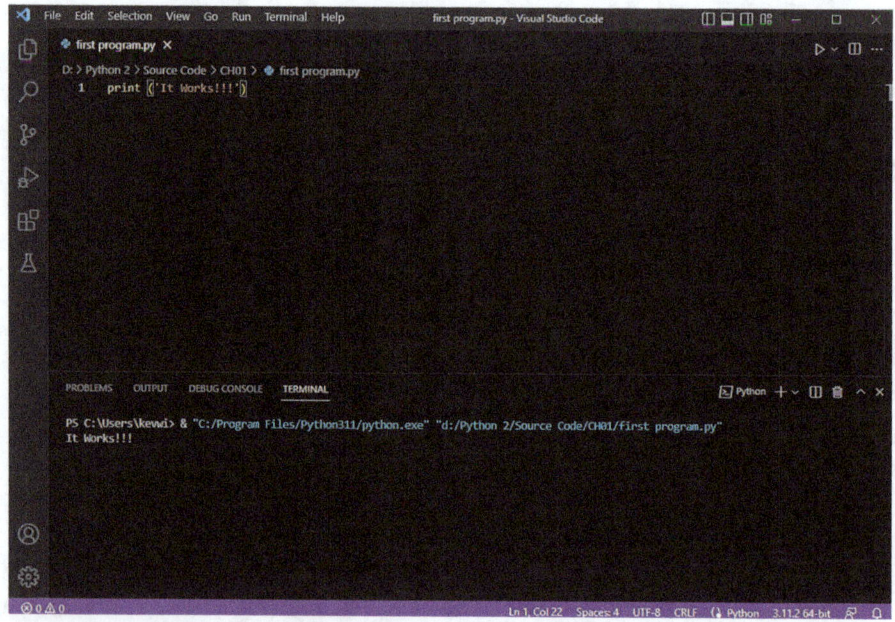

PyCharm

PyCharm is a powerful IDE specifically designed for Python development. You can download the software here:

`www.jetbrains.com/pycharm`

It provides advanced features like intelligent code completion, refactoring tools, debugging, testing frameworks integration, and support for web development frameworks like Django and Flask.

PyCharm is available in both free Community Edition and paid Professional Edition versions.

Sublime Text

Sublime Text is a popular cross-platform code editor known for its speed and simplicity. You can download the software here:

```
www.sublimetext.com
```

It supports Python development through various community-developed packages. Sublime Text offers a distraction-free writing mode, multiple cursors, and powerful search and navigation features.

IDLE

IDLE (Integrated Development and Learning Environment) is a basic Python IDE that comes bundled with the Python installation. It provides a simple and beginner-friendly environment for writing and running Python code.

While IDLE is a convenient option for beginners or when you need a lightweight and straightforward development environment, however it lacks some advanced features and customization options compared to other IDEs. As your Python programming skills and projects become more complex, you may want to explore other IDEs mentioned earlier to leverage additional functionalities and tools for efficient development.

Jupyter Notebook

Jupyter Notebook is an open-source web-based interactive computing environment that allows users to create and share documents called notebooks. To install jupyter notebook, open the command prompt, then run the following command.

```
pip install jupyter
```

Run the following command to run Jupyter Notebook.

```
jupyter notebook
```

Notebook will pop up in your web browser. If it doesn't open your browser and navigate to

```
http://localhost:8888/tree
```

You'll land on the jupyter page.

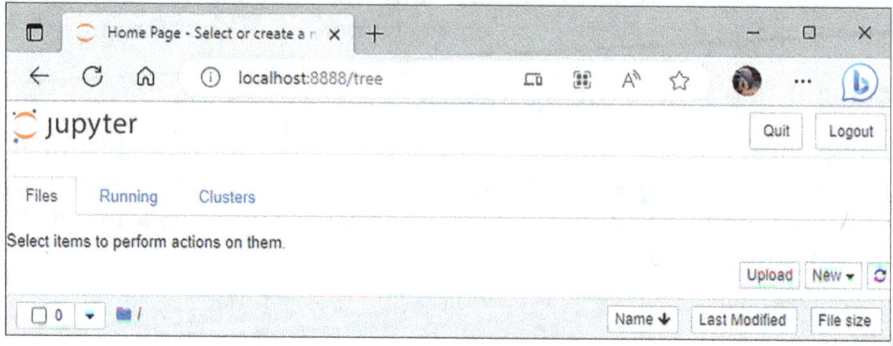

Anaconda is a popular Python distribution that comes bundled with Jupyter Notebook. You can download this here.

```
www.anaconda.com/products/individual
```

Once you download the installer, run through the setup process.

You'll find Anaconda Navigator, and Anaconda Spyder. Anaconda Navigator allows you to create and manage isolated Python environments, switch between different versions of Python, and install/uninstall packages. Spyder is an integrated development environment specifically designed for scientific Python programming and data analysis. It provides a powerful and feature-rich environment for writing, testing, and debugging Python code.

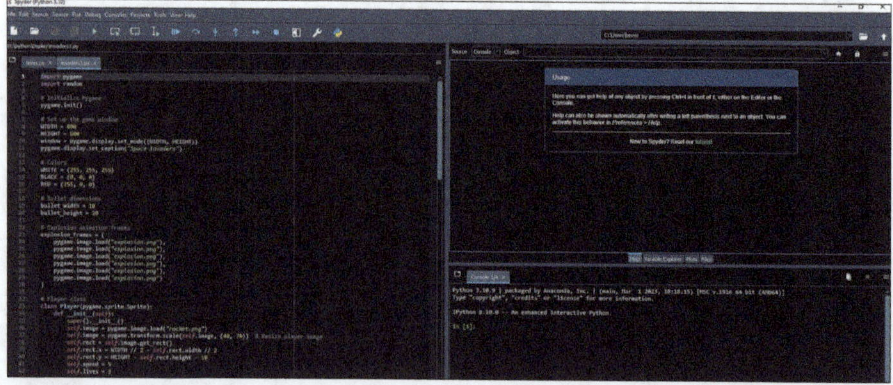

Summary

- Python is a high-level programming language created by Guido van Rossum in 1991, known for its readability and concise syntax.
- Python has a comprehensive library that includes built-in modules and functions for common programming tasks, reducing the need for third-party libraries.
- Python is versatile and widely used in web development, data analysis, artificial intelligence, scientific computing, and automation.
- Code editors such as Visual Studio Code and Sublime Text offer lightweight tools for editing code.
- Integrated Development Environments (IDEs) such as PyCharm, IDLE, and Eclipse provide additional features like debugging, code refactoring, and project management.
- Visual Studio Code is recommended in the book, with excellent Python support, debugging tools, and a wide range of extensions.
- PyCharm is a powerful IDE specifically designed for Python development, available in both free and paid versions.
- Sublime Text is a popular cross-platform code editor with support for Python development through community-developed packages.
- IDLE is a basic Python IDE bundled with the Python installation, suitable for beginners or lightweight development but lacking advanced features.
- Jupyter Notebook is an open-source web-based interactive computing environment that allows users to create and share documents called notebooks.
- Anaconda is a popular Python distribution that comes bundled with Jupyter Notebook.

2

Python Basics

Python is an interpreted programming language, meaning the source code is executed line by line at runtime without the need for prior compilation into machine code.

When you run a Python program, the interpreter translates the source code into bytecode which is then executed by the Python Virtual Machine (PVM). The PVM is responsible for executing the bytecode and managing the memory, objects, and other runtime aspects of the Python program.

Python's appeal lies in its simplicity and readability. The syntax emphasizes code clarity, using indentation rather than traditional braces or keywords to delimit blocks of code.

For this chapter, you'll need to download the source code files from:

`elluminetpress.com/pyb`

You'll also find various video demos and tutorials.

Language Syntax

Syntax refers to the set of rules and structure that define the correct arrangement and usage of elements in a programming language. The rules specify how the code should be structured, including the order and placement of keywords, operators, variables, and other elements. Adhering to the syntax rules is crucial because even small deviations can result in code that produces syntax errors.

Reserved Words

Reserved words, also known as keywords, are words that have special meaning and are reserved for specific purposes. These words cannot be used as variable names or other identifiers because they are already used by the language itself.

Reserved Word	Meaning/Purpose
and	Logical operator for performing a logical AND operation
as	Used in context managers or aliasing
assert	Used to test if a given condition is true
break	Used to exit a loop prematurely
class	Used to define a class in object-oriented programming
continue	Used to skip the current iteration of a loop
def	Used to define a function
del	Used to delete a reference to an object
elif	Used with if statements to define additional conditions
else	Used with if statements or loops to define alternate behavior
except	Catches and handles exceptions
FALSE	Boolean value representing false
finally	Used in exception handling to define code that always executes
for	Used to iterate over a sequence (e.g., list, string)
from	Used in import statements to specify the source module
global	Declares a global variable
if	Used to define a conditional statement
import	Used to import modules or specific attributes from modules
in	Used to test if a value is present in a sequence
is	Used for identity comparison
lambda	Used to create anonymous functions
None	Represents the absence of a value
nonlocal	Declares a variable from an outer (non-global) scope
not	Logical operator for performing a logical NOT operation
or	Logical operator for performing a logical OR operation
pass	Placeholder statement that does nothing
raise	Raises an exception
return	Used to return a value from a function
TRUE	Boolean value representing true
try	Begins a block of code for exception handling
while	Used to create a loop that continues until a condition is met
with	Used to manage context for resources (e.g., file handling)
yield	Used in generator functions to produce a value

Indentation

Python uses indentation to define code blocks instead of using braces or keywords like "begin" and "end" as in other languages. Code blocks are usually indented using spaces or tabs (eg use four spaces per indentation level).

Consistent indentation is crucial in Python because it determines the grouping and hierarchy of code. It is important to note that mixing spaces and tabs for indentation can lead to errors, so it's best to choose one and stick to it. In the example below, notice how the indentation is used to define the code blocks within the greet function. See page 93 for information on defining functions.

```
def greet(name):
    if len(name) > 0:
        print("Hello, " + name + "!")
    else:
        print("Hello there!")
    print("Nice to meet you.")

greet("Alice")
greet("Bob")
greet("")
```

The lines of code inside the if and else blocks are indented, indicating that they are part of those blocks. See page 45 for more information on if statements.

```
def greet(name):
    if len(name) > 0:
        print("Hello, " + name + "!")
    else:
        print("Hello there!")
    print("Nice to meet you.")
```

The line that prints "Nice to meet you" is indented at the same level as the if and else blocks, indicating that it is executed after the conditional statements.

See 'conditional statements' later in this chapter for more information on if-else statements.

Comments

Comments are used to provide explanatory notes or documentation within the code. They are ignored by the Python interpreter and do not affect the execution of the program.

Comments help explain the purpose and functionality of code. They provide additional information for other programmers (and yourself) to understand what the code does, how it works, and why certain decisions were made during its implementation. Well-placed comments can significantly enhance the clarity and readability of code.

You can add single line comments using hash #

```
# This is a single-line comment
```

Or you can add multi line comments. To do this enclose your comments in triple quotes """

```
"""
This is a multi-line comment.
It can span across multiple lines
and is enclosed by triple quotes.
"""
```

Comments also facilitate code maintenance and collaboration. When multiple developers work on a project, comments help communication and understanding of each other's code. They provide a way to leave notes, suggestions, or explanations for future modifications or bug fixes, making it easier for developers to work together effectively.

Comments are often used to temporarily disable or comment out blocks of code during development or debugging. This can be useful when testing alternative code paths, isolating issues, or removing sections of code without permanently deleting them. However, it's important to avoid leaving commented-out code in production codebases, as it can confuse and clutter the codebase over time.

Many Python projects and organizations follow specific commenting guidelines or style guides to ensure consistency across the codebase.

Some popular style guides, such as PEP 8 (Python Enhancement Proposal), provide recommendations for commenting conventions, including the use of sentence case or imperative mood for comments, appropriate line lengths, and formatting guidelines. You can find more information this here:

peps.python.org/pep-0008

Dynamic and Duck Typing

Duck typing is a concept in programming that focuses on the behavior of objects rather than their specific types. The term "duck typing" comes from the saying, "If it looks like a duck, swims like a duck, and quacks like a duck, then it probably is a duck". This principle promotes flexibility and code reuse, as it allows objects of different types to be used interchangeably as long as they exhibit the expected behavior. Here's an example of a duck typed function. See chapter 7 on page 116 for more information on classes, methods and objects.

```
class Duck:
    def quack(self):
        print("Quack! I am a duck.")

class Goose:
    def quack(self):
        print("Quack! I am a goose.")
```

Here we define two classes, Duck and Goose, representing different types of birds. Both classes have a quack() method that prints a specific message representing the sound of the bird.

In the make_quack(animal) function, the animal parameter is treated using duck typing principles.

```
def make_quack(animal):
    if hasattr(animal, 'quack'): animal.quack()
    else:
        print("This animal doesn't quack.")
```

Instead of checking the object's type or class, the function checks if the animal object has a quack method using hasattr(). This allows any object that has a quack() method to be considered suitable for making a quacking sound.

The make_quack() function can be called with different objects that have a quack() method.

```
make_quack(duck)     # Output: Quack! I am a duck.
make_quack(goose)    # Output: Quack! I am a goose.
```

Dynamic typing refers to the characteristic of a programming language where the type of a variable is determined and checked during runtime.

For example, in Python, variables are not explicitly declared with types. Instead, their types are inferred from the assigned values.

```
x = 5              # x is an integer
x = "Hello"        # x is now a string
x = [1, 2, 3]      # x is now a list
```

Here, the variable x is dynamically typed, and its type can change as different values are assigned to it. The type of x is determined at runtime based on the type of the assigned value.

Lab Exercises 2.1

1. What is syntax in programming, and why is it important to adhere to syntax rules?
2. What are reserved words or keywords in Python? Why can't they be used as variable names or identifiers?
3. Identify three reserved words in Python and explain their purpose.
4. How does Python use indentation to define code blocks? Why is consistent indentation important?
5. Write a code snippet that demonstrates the use of indentation to define code blocks in Python.
6. What is the purpose of comments in programming? How do they enhance code clarity and readability?
7. How can comments facilitate code maintenance and collaboration in a team setting?
8. Why would you temporarily disable or comment out blocks of code during development or debugging? What should be avoided when using commented-out code in production codebases?

Basic Input & Output

Basic input and output operations allow your program to interact with the user, read data from external sources, and display results. In Python, there are several ways to handle input and output.

Here, we'll take a look at the print() function and the input() function.

Displaying Output

The print() function is commonly used to display output to the console. You can pass one or more arguments to the print() function.

```
print("This is some text to print")
```

Or you can concatenate different variables to print to the console.

```
print("Name: " + name + ", Age: " + str(age))
```

Accepting Input

The input() function is used to accept user input from the console. This function prompts the user with a message and waits for input.

```
name = input("Enter your name: ")
```

The input is returned as a string, so you may need to convert it to the desired data type. Here, we're converting the string input to an integer.

```
age = int(input("Enter age: "))
```

Lab Exercises 2.2

1. What function do you use to get data from the user?
2. What function do you use to print data to the console?
3. Write a program that asks the user for their name and prints a welcome message using their name.

Variables and Data Types

Variables are used to store data values and have a data type associated with them. This determines the kind of data that can be stored and the operations that can be performed on that data.

These variables act as containers that hold information that can be used and manipulated in the program.

Numeric Data Types

Numeric data types are used to represent numbers and perform mathematical operations in your programs.

Integers

An integer is a data type used to represent whole numbers without any fractional or decimal parts. Integers can be positive, negative, or zero. They are used for a wide range of purposes, including counting, indexing, and performing mathematical calculations. For example

```
age = 25
```

Floats

A float, short for "floating-point number," is a data type used to represent real numbers with fractional parts. Floats are used to perform mathematical calculations that involve decimal values. They are commonly used in scientific and mathematical computations, as well as in applications that require precision and accuracy in representing fractional quantities.

```
height = 1.75
```

Strings

Strings are used to represent sequences of characters. They are commonly used to store and manipulate textual data such as words, sentences, and sometimes even entire documents. You can enclose a string in single quotes (') or double quotes (""). For example.

```
name = "John"
```

Concatenation

String concatenation is the process of combining or joining two or more strings together to create a single string. In Python, you can concatenate strings using the concatenation operator (+) or by using the str() function.

Lets take a look at an example.

Here, we are concatenating the values of the name and age variables with other strings to form the message string.

```
name = "John"
age = 25
message = "My name is " + name + " and I am "
            + str(age)
```

Indexing

You can access individual characters within a string by using the character's position or index. String indexing starts from 0, where the first character is at index 0, the second character is at index 1, and so on.

You can use square brackets [] along with the index value to retrieve a specific character from a string.

In the following example, we have a string variable message that contains the text "Hello, World!".

```
message = "HELLO, WORLD!"
print(message[7])
```

We use indexing to access individual characters from the string.

For example, message[7] retrieves the character at index 7, which is 'W'.

0	1	2	3	4	5	6	7	8	9	10	11	12
H	E	L	L	O	,		W	O	R	L	D	!

You can also use negative indexing to access characters from the end of the string.

The last character is accessed using index -1, the second-to-last character using -2, and so on.

```
message = "HELLO, WORLD!"
print(message[-3])
```

message[-3] retrieves the third-to-last character, which is 'L'.

-13	-12	-11	-10	-9	-8	-7	-6	-5	-4	-3	-2	-1
H	E	L	L	O	,		W	O	R	L	D	!

String indexing allows you to extract specific characters from a string, manipulate them, or use them in various operations. It is an essential concept when working with individual characters within strings.

Slicing Strings

Refers to the process of extracting a portion of a string to create a new string that contains the selected characters. With slicing, you can specify a range of indices to extract multiple characters from a string. The syntax for slicing a string is:

```
string[start:end:step]
```

Where **start** is the index of the first character to include.

Where **end** is the index of the first character to exclude,

Where **step** is the increment between characters.

For example consider the following lines of code.

```
message = "HELLO, WORLD!"

print(message[0:5])
```

Here we slice from index 0 to 4 (excluding 5), retrieving the substring "Hello".

0	1	2	3	4	5	6	7	8	9	10	11	12
H	E	L	L	O	,		W	O	R	L	D	!

Slicing allows you to extract substrings from a string based on specified indices. It provides flexibility in working with different portions of a string, enabling you to manipulate or use specific parts as needed.

You can also use negative indices for slicing, similar to string indexing. Negative indices count from the end of the string. For example

```
message = "HELLO, WORLD!"

print(message[-6:-1])
```

In this example, message[-6:-1] slices from index -6 to -2 (excluding -1), retrieving the substring "World".

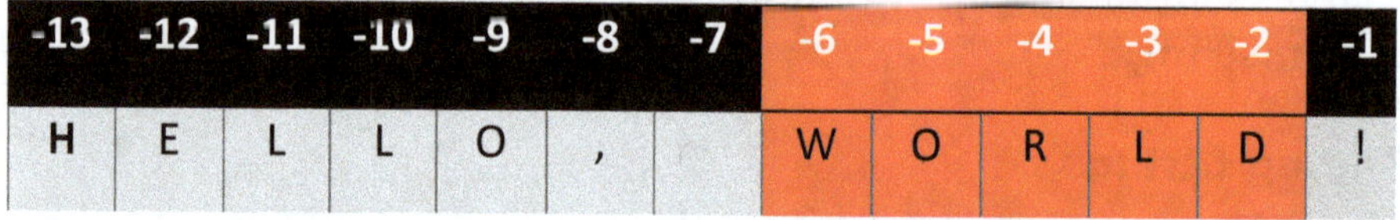

Negative indexing is a powerful feature that allows you to access characters from the end of a string without knowing its length.

Formatting Strings

Formatting strings allows you to create dynamic and formatted output by combining variables and other values into a string. Python provides several ways to format strings. You can use the str.format() method, f-strings (formatted string literals), and the older % operator.

Using the str.format() method, you can embed variables or values into a string by using placeholders {}. You can then pass the values to the format() method to replace the placeholders with the actual values. For example

```
name = "Alice"

age = 30

message = "My name is {} and I am {} years old".
          format(name, age)

print(message)
```

This will output

```
My name is Alice and I am 30 years old
```

In this example, we use {} as a placeholder in the string. When the format() method is called with the values name and age passed as arguments. The placeholders {} are replaced with the actual values in the string.

You can also format a string using f-strings (formatted string literals). F-strings are a newer and more concise way of formatting strings introduced in Python 3.6. They allow you to embed expressions directly into string literals by using the f prefix. You can enclose the expressions within curly braces {}. For example

```
name = "Alice"

age = 30

message = f"My name is {name} and I am {age} years
          old"

print(message)
```

In this example, we use f-strings to directly embed the values of the variables name and age into the string. The variables within the curly braces {} are evaluated and replaced with the values of these variables when the string is created.

Escape Characters

An escape character tells the interpreter to perform a specific operation such as a line break or tab or a reserved character such as a quote mark or apostrophe. Escape characters start with the a backslash (\) and are used to format a string.

Escape Character	Function
\n	Line break
\t	Tab (horizontal indentation)
\	New line in a multi-line string
\\	Backslash
\'	Apostrophe or single quote
\"	Double quote

For example, you could use the tab escape and break line character to format some text.

```
print("John \t 45 \nJoanne \t 15")
```

The output to this line would look something like this:

```
John     45

Joanne   15
```

String Methods

Python provides a variety of string methods that allow you to manipulate and perform operations on strings.

Here are some commonly used string methods:

1. **.len()** returns the length of a string.

   ```
   message = "Hello, World!"
   print(len(message))
   ```

2. **.lower()** converts a string to lowercase.

   ```
   message = "Hello, World!"
   print(message.lower())
   ```

3. **.upper()** converts a string to uppercase.

   ```
   message = "Hello, World!"
   print(message.upper())
   ```

4. **.islower()** checks if all characters in a string are lowercase. Can also use .isupper() to check if all characters in string are uppercase.

   ```
   message = "hello, world!"
   print(message.islower())
   ```

5. **.strip()** removes leading and trailing whitespace from a string.

   ```
   message = "   Hello, World!    "
   print(message.strip())
   ```

6. **.split()** splits a string into a list of substrings based on a delimiter.

```
message = "Hello, World!"
words = message.split(", ")
print(words)
```

7. **.join()** joins a list of strings into a single string, using a specified delimiter.

```
words = ['Hello', 'World!']
message = ", ".join(words)
print(message)
```

8. **.replace()** replaces occurrences of a substring with another substring.

```
message = "Hello, World!"
new_message = message.replace("Hello", "Hi")
print(new_message)
```

9. **.startswith()** checks if a string starts with a specified substring.

```
message = "Hello, World!"
print(message.startswith("Hello"))
```

10. **.endswith()** checks if a string ends with a specified substring.

```
message = "Hello, World!"
print(message.endswith("World!"))
```

11. **.find()** searches for the first occurrence of a substring in a string and returns its index. Returns -1 if not found.

```
message = "Hello, World!"
print(message.find("World"))
```

12. **.count()** counts the number of occurrences of a substring within a string

```
message = "Hello, World!"
print(message.count("o"))
```

What happens when you execute these pieces of code? Give them a try. Have a look at stringmethods.py

Boolean Data Type

Also known as logical operators and are commonly used in conditional statements (if...) or constructing loops (while... for...). We'll look at if statements, and loops on page 45.

Operator	Description
and	Returns true if both the operands are true
or	Returns true if either of the operands is true
not	Returns true if operand is false

For example, you could join to two comparisons in an 'if' statement using 'and', like this:

```
if a >= 0 and a <= 10:

   print ("Your number is between 0 and 10")

else

   print ("Out of range - must be between 0 & 10")
```

Using the 'and' operator would mean both conditions (a >= 0) and (a <= 10) must be true.

Lab Exercises 2.3

1. What are variables, and what role do they play in programming?
2. Explain the difference between integers and floats in Python. Give an example of each.
3. What are strings, and how are they commonly used in programming? Provide an example of a string.
4. What is string concatenation, and how can it be achieved in Python?
5. How can you access individual characters within a string using indexing? Give an example.
6. How does string slicing work in Python? Provide an example of slicing a string.

7. Explain the concept of string formatting and provide two methods to format strings in Python.
8. List three commonly used string methods in Python and briefly explain their purposes.
9. What is the boolean data type in Python, and what are its possible values?
10. Create a variable called "age" and assign it an integer value representing your age.
11. Create a variable called "height" and assign it a float value representing your height.
12. Create a variable called "name" and assign it a string value representing your name.
13. Concatenate the "name" and "age" variables to create a message introducing yourself. Print the message.
14. Access the third character of the string "Hello, World!" using indexing.
15. Slice the string "Python Programming" to create a new string containing only "Programming". Print the new string.
16. Use string formatting to create a message that includes the values of the variables "name" and "height". Print the message.
17. Use the .upper() method to convert the string "hello" to uppercase and print the result.
18. Use the .replace() method to replace all occurrences of the letter "a" in the string "banana" with the letter "e". Print the result.
19. Check if the string "Hello, World!" starts with the substring "Hello" using the .startswith() method. Print the result.
20. Create a boolean variable called "is_raining" and assign it a value of False.

Operators and Expressions

Operators perform specific operations on one or more operands (values or variables).

Arithmetic Operators

Arithmetic operators are used with numeric data types such as integers and floats.

Operator	Description
Addition (+)	Adds two operands.
Subtraction (-)	Subtracts the second operand from the first.
Multiplication (*)	Multiplies two operands.
Division (/)	Divides the first operand by the second.
Modulo (%)	Returns the remainder of the division.
Exponentiation (**)	Raises the first operand to the power of the second.

They are commonly used in mathematical expressions and computations in various scientific, and financial applications.

Performing Arithmetic

If you wanted to add 20% sales tax to a price of $12.95, you could do something like this...

```
total = 12.95 + 12.95 * 20 / 100
```

According to the precedence list above, you would first evaluate the 'divide' operator:

```
20 / 100 = 0.2
```

Next is multiply

```
12.95 * 0.2 = 2.59
```

Finally addition

```
12.95 + 2.59 = 15.54
```

Comparison Operators

Comparison operators are used to compare two values or expressions in Python. They return a Boolean value (True or False) based on the comparison result.

Operator	Description
And	Returns True if both operands are True.
Or	Returns True if either operand is True.
Not	Returns the opposite boolean value of the operand.

These comparison operators are often used in conditional statements, loops, and other control structures to make decisions based on the comparison results.

Assignment Operators

Assignment operators are used to assign values to variables. They also allow you to modify the value of a variable by performing an operation and assigning the result back to the variable.

Operator	Description
Assignment (=)	Assigns a value to a variable.
Addition assignment (+=)	Adds a value to the variable and assigns the result.
Subtraction assignment (-=)	Subtracts a value from the variable and assigns the result.
Multiplication assignment (*=)	Multiplies the variable by a value and assigns the result.
Division assignment (/=)	Divides the variable by a value and assigns the result.
Modulo assignment (%=)	Performs modulo operation on the variable and assigns the result.

Making Expressions

We can use these operators to write expressions. Expressions are combinations of operators, variables, and values that evaluate to a single value.

Expressions are formed by using operators to operate on operands that represent computations or evaluations.

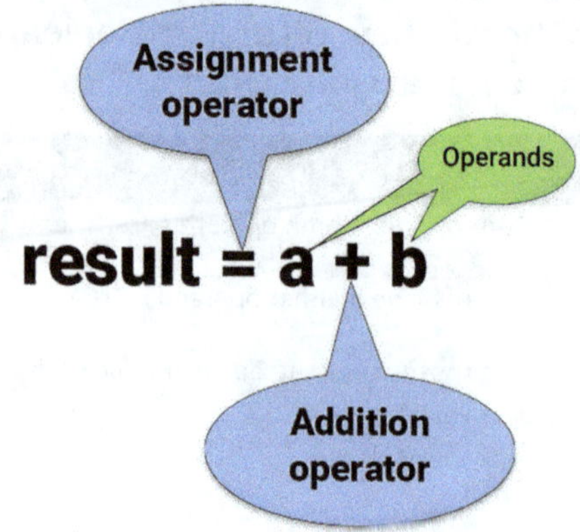

Here **a** and **b** are the operands.

Operator Precedence

BIDMAS (sometimes called BODMAS) is an acronym commonly used to remember mathematical operator precedence - ie the order in which you evaluate each operator.

Here in the table below we see the arithmetic operators (BIDMAS), followed by bitwise, comparison then the logical operators.

	Operator	Description
B	Parentheses	()
I	Exponentiation	**
D	Unary plus and minus	+x, -x
M	Multiplication, division,	*, /, //, %
A	and modulo	
S	Addition and subtraction	+, -
Bitwise	Bitwise shift operators	<<, >>
	Bitwise AND	&
	Bitwise XOR	^
	Bitwise OR	`
Comp	Comparison operators	<, <=, >, >=, ==, !=
Logical	Logical NOT	not
	Logical AND	and
	Logical OR	or

Type Casting

Type casting refers to the process of converting a variable from one data type to another. Variables can contain various types of data such as text (called a string), a whole number (called an integer), or a floating point number (numbers with decimal points). With Python, you don't have to declare all your variables before you use them. However, you might need to convert variables to different types. This is known as type casting.

Python has two types of type conversion: implicit & explicit.

With implicit type conversion, Python automatically converts one data type to another.

With explicit type conversion, the programmer converts the data type to the required data type using a specific function. You can the following functions to cast your data types:

- **int( )** converts data to an integer
- **long( )** converts data to a long integer
- **float( )** converts data to a floating point number
- **str( )** converts data to a string

For example, you could use the input( ) function to prompt the user for some data

```
a = input ('Enter first number: ')
```

This example would prompt the user for some data, then store the data in the 'a' variable as a string.

This might sound ok, but what if we wanted to perform some arithmetic on the data? We can't do that if the data is stored as a string. We'd have to explicitly type cast the data in the variable as an integer or a float.

```
int(a)
```

or

```
float(a)
```

Lab Exercises 2.4

1. What are arithmetic, comparison and assignment operators? Show examples.

2. Write an expression that adds two variables, x and y, and assigns the result to a variable sum_result.

3. Create an expression that multiplies the variables a and b, subtracts the variable c, and assigns the result to the variable result.

4. Write an expression that checks if the value of the variable age is greater than or equal to 18 and assigns the Boolean result to the variable is_adult.

5. Create an expression that checks if the length of the string variable name is greater than 5 and assigns the Boolean result to the variable is_long_name.

6. Write an expression that calculates the remainder when the variable numerator is divided by the variable denominator and assigns the result to the variable remainder.

7. Create an expression that checks if the variable x is equal to 10 or the variable y is equal to 20 and assigns the Boolean result to the variable is_valid.

8. Write an expression that converts the string variable num_str to an integer using the int() function and assigns the result to the variable num.

9. Create an expression that converts the floating-point variable pi to a string using the str() function and assigns the result to the variable pi_str.

10. Write an expression that converts the integer variable is_valid to a Boolean using the bool() function and assigns the result to the variable is_valid_bool.

11. Create an expression that converts the list variable numbers to a tuple using the tuple() function and assigns the result to the variable numbers_tuple.

12. What is type casting?

Conditional Statements

Conditional statements are used to execute different blocks of code based on certain conditions. These statements allow the program to make decisions and choose different paths of execution based on whether a specific condition is true or false.

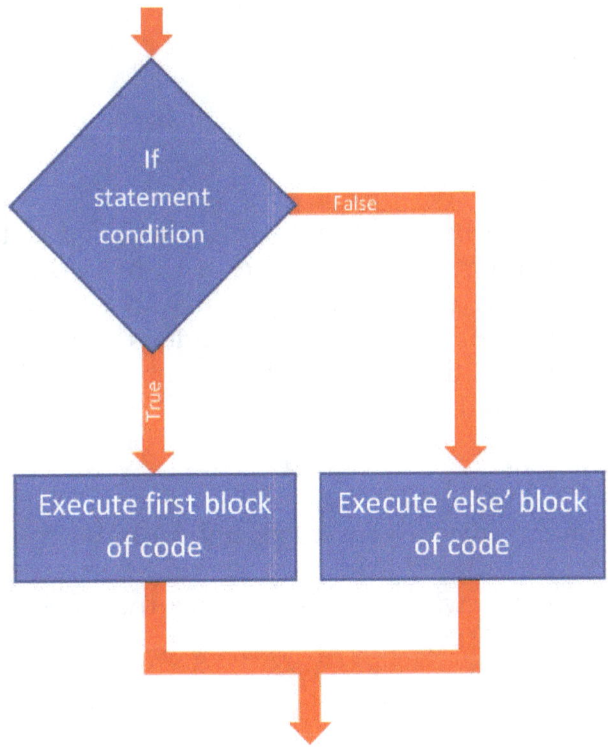

If Statement

The if statement is used to execute a block of code if a specified condition is true. If the condition evaluates to true, the indented block of code beneath the if statement is executed. If the condition is false, the block of code is skipped, and the program moves on to the next statement after the if statement.

```
x = 5

if x > 0:

    print("x is positive")
```

If...Else

The if-else statement allows you to specify two blocks of code: one to execute if a certain condition is true, and another to execute if the condition is false

```
num = 10

if num % 2 == 0:
    print("The number is even.")

else:
    print("The number is odd.")
```

In this example, we have a variable num with the value of 10. The condition num % 2 == 0 checks if num is divisible by 2 without a remainder (this determines it's an even number). If the condition is true, the code block under the if statement is executed. If the condition is false, the code block under the else statement is executed.

Elif Statement

The elif statement allows you to specify multiple conditions to be evaluated sequentially and provides an alternative to using nested if statements when you have more than two conditions to evaluate.

Lets take a look at an example

```
score = 85

if score >= 90:
    grade = "A"

elif score >= 80:
    grade = "B"

elif score >= 70:
    grade = "C"

elif score >= 60:
    grade = "D"

else:
    grade = "Fail"
```

Here, the code checks the value of score against multiple conditions using multiple elif statements.

The first if statement checks to see if the score is greater than or equal to 90. If true, the code assigns the "A" to the grade variable.

If the score is not greater than or equal to 90, the code moves to the next elif condition. If the score is greater than or equal to 80, it assigns the "B" to the grade variable.

If the score is not greater than or equal to 80, the code moves to the next elif condition. If the score is greater than or equal to 70, it assigns the "C" to the grade variable.

If the score is not greater than or equal to 70, the code moves to the next elif condition. If the score is greater than or equal to 60, it assigns the "D" to the grade variable.

If none of the above conditions are met, meaning the score is less than 60, the code executes the else condition and assigns "Fail" to the grade variable.

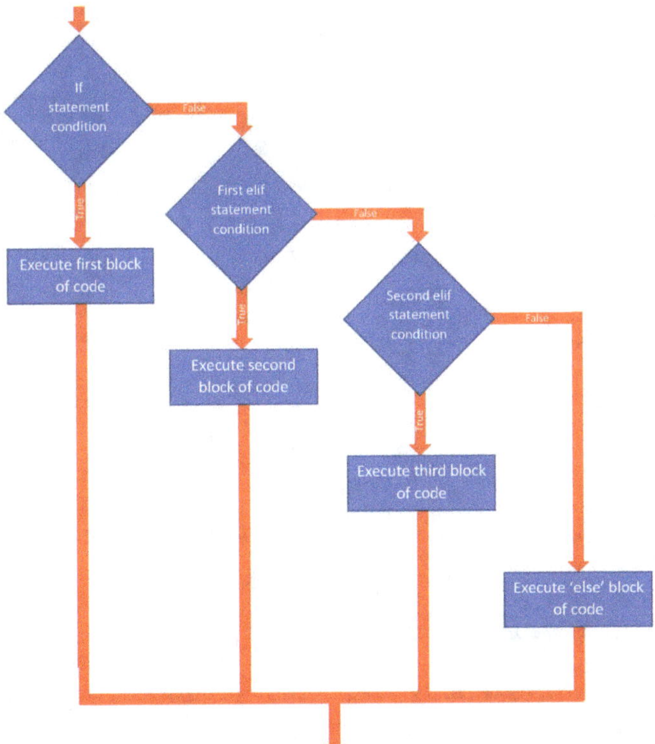

Nested If Statements

By nesting if statements, you can create more complex decision-making logic. It allows you to handle multi-level conditions and execute specific code blocks based on the combination of those conditions. This nesting can be done with if statements, and elif statements. In this example we've nested the elif and if statements.

```
weight = float(input("Enter the weight kilograms: "))
destination = input("Enter the destination: ")

if weight <= 0:
    print("Invalid weight.")

elif destination == "domestic":
    if weight <= 1:
        print("Shipping cost: $5")

    elif weight <= 5:
        print("Shipping cost: $10")

    elif weight <= 10:
        print("Shipping cost: $15")

    else:
        print("Shipping cost: $20")

elif destination == "international":
    if weight <= 1:
        print("Shipping cost: $15")

    elif weight <= 5:
        print("Shipping cost: $25")

    elif weight <= 10:
        print("Shipping cost: $40")

    else:
        print("Shipping cost: $60")

else:
    print("Invalid destination.")
```

Have a look at nestedifs.py

Lab Exercises 2.5

1. Write a program that prompts the user to enter their age and prints "You are an adult" if the age is 18 or older, and "You are a minor" otherwise.

2. Write a program that takes a number as input and determines if it is positive, negative, or zero. If the number is greater than 0, print "Positive." If the number is less than 0, print "Negative." If the number is equal to 0, print "Zero."

3. Write a program that checks if a given year is a leap year. If the year is evenly divisible by 4 and not divisible by 100, or if it is divisible by 400, print "Leap year." Otherwise, print "Not a leap year."

4. Write a program that asks the user to enter a grade (a number between 0 and 100) and prints the corresponding letter grade. Use the following grading scale: 90 and above - "A", 80-89 - "B", 70-79 - "C", 60-69 - "D", below 60 - "F".

5. Write a program that takes three numbers as input and finds the maximum among them. Print the maximum number.

6. Write a program that prompts the user to enter a month (as a number from 1 to 12) and prints the corresponding month name. Use an if-elif-else statement to handle each case.

7. Write a program that checks if a given string is a palindrome. A palindrome is a word or phrase that reads the same backward as forward. If the string is a palindrome, print "Palindrome." Otherwise, print "Not a palindrome."

8. Write a program that determines if a given number is divisible by both 3 and 5. If the number is divisible by both, print "Divisible by 3 and 5." Otherwise, print "Not divisible by 3 and 5."

9. Write a program that calculates the discount for a shopping cart based on the total amount. If the total amount is greater than or equal to $100, apply a 10% discount. If the total amount is greater than or equal to $50 but less than $100, apply a 5% discount. If the total amount is less than $50, no discount is applied. Print the discounted amount.

10. Write a program that determines if a given year is a leap year or a century leap year. A century leap year occurs every 100 years and is only a leap year if it is divisible by 400. If the year is a leap year, print "Leap year." If it is a century leap year, print "Century leap year." Otherwise, print "Not a leap year or century leap year."

Iteration

Iteration refers to the process of repeatedly executing a block of code until a certain condition is met and is a fundamental concept in programming used extensively to process collections of data, perform calculations, and execute repetitive tasks. Python provides several constructs for iteration, including loops and iterators.

For Loop

A for loop is a control flow statement that allows you to iterate over a sequence (such as a list, tuple, string, or range) or any object that is iterable.

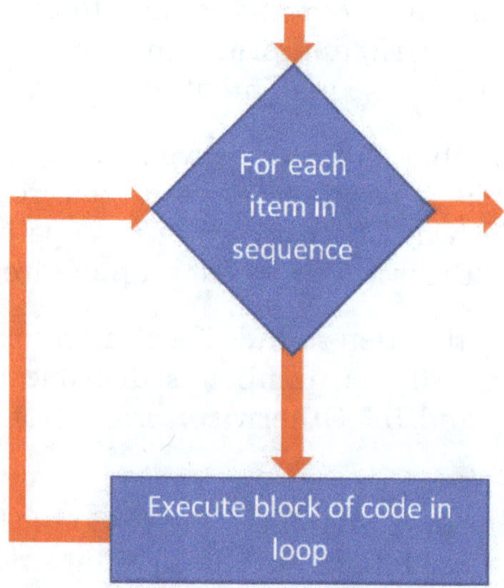

It is commonly used when you know the number of iterations in advance or when you want to iterate over the elements of a sequence.

Lets take a look at an example

```
fruits = ["apple", "banana", "cherry"]

for fruit in fruits:
    print(fruit)
```

In this example, the for loop iterates over the fruits list, assigning each element to the fruit variable in each iteration. The print(fruit) statement within the loop prints each fruit to the console.

While Loop

The while loop is a control flow statement that allows you to repeatedly execute a block of code as long as a specified condition is true.

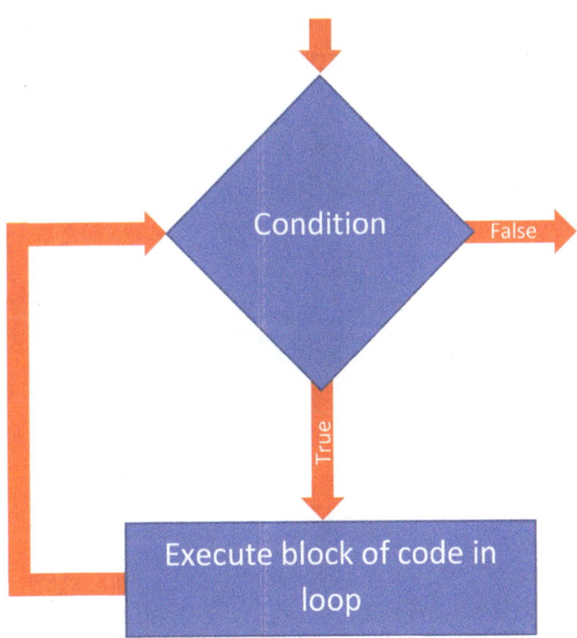

It is used when you want to perform a task repeatedly until a certain condition is met or until a termination condition is encountered.

It provides flexibility for situations where the number of iterations is not known in advance or when you want to repeat a task until a specific condition is met.

Lets take a look at an example.

Here, the while loop starts with i initialized to 1. The loop continues executing the code block as long as i is less than or equal to 5. In each iteration, the value of i is printed, and then i is incremented by 1 using i += 1.

```
i = 1

while i <= 5:
    print(i)
    i += 1
```

Break and Continue Statements

The break statement is commonly used to exit a loop when a certain condition is met or when you want to stop iterating based on some criteria. It is particularly useful for avoiding unnecessary iterations and improving efficiency.

The continue statement is used to skip the rest of the code block for the current iteration and move on to the next iteration of the loop. It allows you to selectively bypass certain parts of the loop's code block.

```
i = 0

while i < 5:
    i += 1
    if i == 3:
        continue
    print(i)
    if i == 4:
        break
```

In this example, the loop starts with i initialized to 0.

The loop continues as long as i is less than 5. Inside the loop, i is incremented by 1.

When i is equal to 3, the continue statement is encountered, skipping the print(i) statement for that iteration (if statement).

When i becomes 4, the break statement is encountered, terminating the loop (if statement).

Looping Over Data

Looping over data structures is a common programming task that involves iterating through the elements of a collection or data structure such as a list.

```
my_list = [2, 5, 7, 8, 9]

for element in my_list:
    print(element)
```

Here, a for loop that iterates over each element in my_list. In each iteration, the current element is assigned to the variable element and printed to the screen.

Nested Loops

A nested loop is a loop inside another loop. This creates a hierarchical structure where the inner loop is nested within the body of the outer loop. Each iteration of the outer loop triggers a complete set of iterations of the inner loop.

```
matrix = [[1, 2, 3],
          [4, 5, 6],
          [7, 8, 9]]

for row in matrix:
    for element in row:
        print(element, end=' ')

    print()
```

The outer loop iterates over each row in the matrix (2D list). The inner loop iterates over each element in the current row.

Iterators and Iterables

Iterators and iterables are concepts related to working with sequences of data. Understanding these concepts is crucial for effective iteration and processing of data in Python. An iterable is any object that can be looped over or iterated. It is an object that contains a collection of elements and supports iteration through those elements.

For example, lists, tuples, strings, dictionaries, and sets. Iterables are generally represented as sequences. You can use a for loop to iterate over an iterable and access its elements one by one. The for loop automatically retrieves the elements from the iterable until there are no more elements left to process.

```
my_list = [1, 2, 3, 4, 5]

for item in my_list:
    print(item)
```

An iterator is an object that implements the iterator protocol, which consists of the __iter__() and __next__() methods. It provides a way to access elements from an iterable one at a time, maintaining the state of iteration. When you use a for loop to iterate over an iterable, it automatically creates an iterator object behind the scenes and calls the __iter__() method to obtain the iterator. Then in each iteration, it calls the __next__() method on the iterator to retrieve the next element.

```
my_list = [1, 2, 3, 4, 5]
my_iter = iter(my_list)
print(next(my_iter))
print(next(my_iter))
print(next(my_iter))
```

The next() function retrieves the next element from the iterator. If there are no more elements, it raises a StopIteration exception. The key difference between an iterable and an iterator is that an iterable is an object that can be iterated over. An iterator is an object that actually performs the iteration and keeps track of the current state.

Lab Exercises 2.6

1. Write a program that uses a for loop to iterate over a list of numbers and prints each number multiplied by 2.

2. Write a program that asks the user to enter a string and uses a while loop to print each character of the string in reverse order.

3. Write a program that uses a for loop to iterate over a string and counts the number of vowels (a, e, i, o, u) in the string. Print the total count of vowels.

4. Write a program that prompts the user to enter a series of numbers. Use a while loop to continuously prompt for numbers until the user enters a negative number. Then, print the sum of all the positive numbers entered.

5. Write a program that uses a for loop to iterate over a list of names. If a name starts with the letter 'A', print "Hello, [name]!" Otherwise, print "Greetings, [name]!"

6. Write a program that generates a random number between 1 and 10. Use a while loop to continuously ask the user to guess the number until they guess correctly. Provide feedback on each guess (e.g., "Too high" or "Too low").

7. Write a program that uses a for loop to iterate over a list of words. If a word has more than 5 characters, print the word in uppercase. Otherwise, print the word in lowercase.

8. Write a program that uses a for loop to iterate over a range of numbers from 1 to 10. Print the square of each number.

9. Write a program that asks the user to enter a sentence. Use a for loop to iterate over the words in the sentence and count the number of words that have more than 3 characters. Print the count.

Summary

- Python is an interpreted programming language, and its source code is executed line by line at runtime.
- The Python interpreter translates the source code into bytecode and executes it using the Python Virtual Machine (PVM).
- Language syntax refers to the rules and structure that define the correct arrangement of elements in Python.
- Reserved words or keywords are words with special meanings in Python and cannot be used as variable names or identifiers.
- Python uses indentation to define code blocks instead of braces or keywords like "begin" and "end."

- Comments in Python are used for explanatory notes, documentation, and code clarity. They are ignored by the interpreter.
- Variables are used to store data values and have associated data types (e.g., integers, floats, strings).
- Numeric data types include integers and floats, used for whole numbers and real numbers, respectively.
- Strings represent sequences of characters and can be enclosed in single or double quotes.
- String concatenation combines multiple strings using the concatenation operator (+) or the str() function.
- String indexing and slicing allow accessing specific characters or substrings within a string.
- String formatting provides ways to embed variables and values into strings using placeholders, such as {} or f-strings.
- The bool data type represents boolean values (True or False) in Python.
- Operators perform operations on operands (values or variables).
- Arithmetic operators (+, -, *, /, %, **) perform mathematical calculations on numeric data types.
- Comparison operators (==, !=, >, <, >=, <=) compare two values and return a Boolean result.
- Logical operators (and, or, not) manipulate Boolean values and are used for combining conditions.
- Assignment operators (=, +=, -=, *=, /=, %=) assign values to variables and modify their values.
- Type casting is the process of converting a value from one data type to another. Implicit type casting is performed automatically by Python, while explicit type casting requires specific functions.
- Functions for type casting include int(), float(), str(), bool(), list(), tuple(), set(), and dict().

- Conditional statements are used to execute different blocks of code based on conditions.
  - The if statement executes a block of code if a specified condition is true.
  - The if-else statement executes one block of code if a condition is true and another block if it is false.
  - The elif statement allows for evaluating multiple conditions sequentially.
- Iteration is the process of repeating a block of code until a specific condition is met. Python provides constructs for iteration such as for loops and while loops.
- A for loop is used to iterate over a sequence or any iterable object and is used when the number of iterations is known or when iterating over the elements of a sequence.
- A while loop is used to repeatedly execute a block of code as long as a condition is true and is used when the number of iterations is not known or when repeating a task until a specific condition is met.
- The break statement is used to exit a loop prematurely when a certain condition is met and helps avoid unnecessary iterations and improve efficiency.
- The continue statement is used to skip the current iteration and move on to the next iteration of the loop. It allows selective bypassing of certain parts of the loop's code block.
- An iterable is any object that can be looped over or iterated.
- An iterator is an object that implements the iterator protocol and provides a way to access elements from an iterable one at a time, maintaining the state of iteration.
- Iterators are created from iterables, and the next() function is used to retrieve the next element from an iterator.
- The key difference is that an iterable is the object being iterated over, while an iterator performs the iteration and keeps track of the current state.

3 Data Structures

Data structures are used to organize and store data in a structured manner, hence the name. They provide an efficient way to manage, access, and manipulate data. There are several built-in data structures that cater to different needs, such as lists, tuples, sets and dictionaries.

Some data structures are mutable meaning we can modify them by adding, removing, or changing their elements. Python has three built in mutable data structures: lists, dictionaries, and sets. Immutable data structures cannot be modified after they have been created meaning you can't add new, remove, or replace elements. A tuple is a data structure that is immutable.

For this chapter, you'll need to download the source code files from:

`elluminetpress.com/pyds`

You'll also find various video demos and tutorials.

Lists

Lists are one of the most versatile and widely used data structures in Python. They are ordered, mutable, and can contain elements of different data types. Lists are defined using square brackets [ ] and elements are separated by commas.

```
my_list = ["Bread", "Milk", "Coffee", "Cereal"]
```

Each item in the list is indexed. Remember the index always starts from 0.

So to index items in the list above, we reference it using the index. For example:

```
my_list[2]
```

This will reference "Coffee" as we can see below.

You can assign another value to an item in the list (eg change coffee).

```
my_list[2] = "Chocolate"
```

To insert an item – specify index to insert item at. For example to insert 'grapes' at index 1

```
my_list.insert(1, "grapes")
```

This inserts grape at index[1] and shifts items after insert point to the right.

To remove an item by value

```
my_list.remove('chocolate')
```

This will remove the element 'chocolate' from the list.

Once the item is removed, the items after will shift.

A list is a versatile data structure that provides several built-in methods to manipulate and work with lists. Here are a few common examples:

1. **.append(element)** adds an element to the end of the list.

```
my_list = [1, 2, 3]
my_list.append(4)
print(my_list)
```

2. **.extend(iterable)** appends the elements of an iterable (e.g., another list) to the end of the list.

```
my_list = [1, 2, 3]
my_list.extend([4, 5, 6])
print(my_list)
```

3. **.insert(index, element)** inserts an element at a specified index in the list.

```
my_list = [1, 2, 3]
my_list.insert(1, 10)
print(my_list)
```

4. **.remove(element)** removes the first occurrence of the specified element from the list.

```
my_list = [1, 2, 3, 2, 4]
my_list.remove(2)
print(my_list)
```

5. **.pop(index)** removes and returns the element at the specified index. If no index is provided, it removes and returns the last element.

```
my_list = [1, 2, 3]
popped_element = my_list.pop(1)
print(popped_element)
print(my_list)
```

6. **.index(element)** returns the index of the first occurrence of the specified element in the list.

```
my_list = [1, 2, 3, 2, 4]
index = my_list.index(2)
print(index)
```

7. **.count(element)** returns the number of occurrences of the specified element in the list.

```
my_list = [1, 2, 3, 2, 4]
count = my_list.count(2)
print(count)
```

8. **.sort()** sorts the elements in the list in ascending order.

```
my_list = [3, 1, 4, 2]
my_list.sort()
print(my_list)
```

9. **.reverse()** reverses the order of the elements in the list.

```
my_list = [1, 2, 3]
my_list.reverse()
print(my_list)
```

10. **.copy()** returns a shallow copy of the list.

```
my_list = [1, 2, 3]
new_list = my_list.copy()
print(new_list)
```

Try them out and see what happens.

Have a look at listmethods.py. Study the code to make sure you understand how the methods are used.

2D Lists

A 2D list is a list of lists. It allows you to store data in a tabular form with rows and columns. Each element in a 2D list represents a value at a specific row and column position.

```
my_2d_list = [
    [ 21, 8, 17, 4 ],
    [ 2, 16, 9, 19 ],
    [ 8, 21, 14, 3 ],
    [ 3, 18, 15, 5 ]
]
```

You can visualise this as a grid similar to a table with rows and columns. Each column in the grid is numbered starting with 0.

```
my_2d_list = [
    [ 21, 8, 17, 4 ],
    [ 2, 16, 9, 19 ],
    [ 8, 21, 14, 3 ],
    [ 3, 18, 15, 5 ]
]
```

Each row is numbered starting with 0. Each cell in the grid is identified by an index - the row index followed by the column index as shown as shown in figure 1 below.

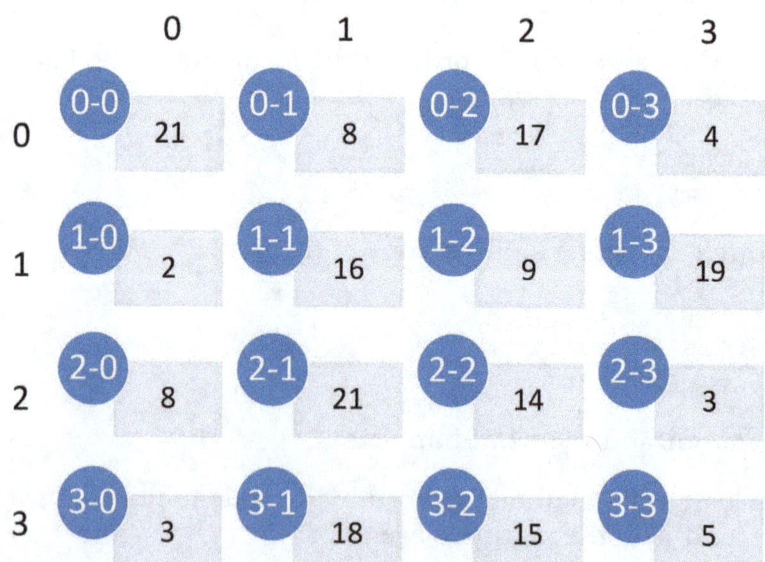

If you want to reference a value in the 2D list, first reference the row index, then the column index. Now what if we wanted to reference the value circled in figure below?

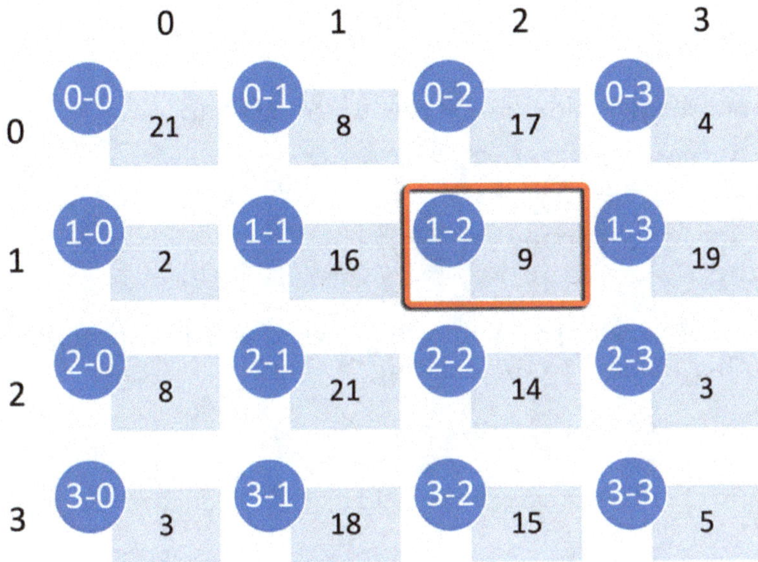

First, we reference the row the value is on.

```
my_2d_list = [1]
```

Then the column

```
my_2d_list = [1][2]
```

When working with 2D lists, you can use a combination of list and nested list methods to manipulate and access the elements. Here are some common methods:

1. **len(list)** returns the number of rows in the 2D list.

```
my_2d_list = [[1, 2, 3], [4, 5, 6], [7, 8, 9]]
rows = len(my_2d_list)
print(rows)  # Output: 3
```

2. **list[row_index]** accesses a specific row in the 2D list.

```
my_2d_list = [[1, 2, 3], [4, 5, 6], [7, 8, 9]]
row = my_2d_list[1]
print(row)  # Output: [4, 5, 6]
```

3. **list[row_index][column_index]** accesses a specific element in the 2D list using row and column indexes.

```
my_2d_list = [[1, 2, 3], [4, 5, 6], [7, 8, 9]]
element = my_2d_list[1][2]
print(element)
```

4. **append(row)** adds a new row to the 2D list.

```
my_2d_list = [[1, 2, 3], [4, 5, 6]]
new_row = [7, 8, 9]
my_2d_list.append(new_row)
print(my_2d_list)
```

5. **extend(iterable)** appends the rows of another iterable (e.g., another 2D list) to the existing 2D list.

```
my_2d_list = [[1, 2, 3], [4, 5, 6]]
other_list = [[7, 8, 9], [10, 11, 12]]
my_2d_list.extend(other_list)
print(my_2d_list)
```

6. **insert(row_index, row)** inserts a new row at the specified row index.

```
my_2d_list = [[1, 2, 3], [4, 5, 6]]
new_row = [7, 8, 9]
my_2d_list.insert(1, new_row)
print(my_2d_list)
```

7. **pop(row_index)** removes and returns the row at the specified row index.

```
my_2d_list = [[1, 2, 3], [4, 5, 6], [7, 8, 9]]
popped_row = my_2d_list.pop(1)
print(popped_row)
```

8. **sort()** sorts the list in ascending order

```
numbers = [5, 2, 8, 1, 3]
numbers.sort()
print(numbers)  # Output: [1, 2, 3, 5, 8]
```

9. **count()** returns the number of occurrences of an element in the list.

```
fruits = ['apple', 'banana', 'cherry', 'banana']
count = fruits.count('banana')
print(count)
```

Have a look at list2dmethods.py. Try them, see what happens.

Lab Exercises 3.1

1. Write a Python program to sum all the elements in a given list.
2. Write a Python program to count the number of even and odd numbers in a given list.
3. Write a Python program to check if a given list is sorted in ascending order.
4. Write a Python program to reverse a given list.
5. Write a Python program to find the frequency of each element in a given list.

Tuples

Tuples are similar to lists but are immutable, meaning their elements cannot be modified once defined. They are commonly used when you need to store a collection of values that should not be changed. Tuples are defined using parentheses ( ) and elements are separated by commas.

```
my_tuple = ("bread", "milk", "coffee", "cereal")
```

Tuples are also indexed meaning you can access individual elements in a similar fashion to lists. Remember the indexing always starts from 0.

If we want to reference an item in the tuple, add the index in square brackets. For example, the following line references "coffee".

```
my_tuple[2]
```

Since tuples are immutable there are a limited number of built-in methods compared to other data structures. Here are a couple of useful methods:

1. **count()** returns the number of occurrences of a specified element in the tuple.

```
my_tuple = (1, 2, 3, 2, 4, 2)
count = my_tuple.count(2)
print(count)
```

2. **index()** returns the index of the first occurrence of a specified element in the tuple.

```
my_tuple = ('a', 'b', 'c', 'a', 'd')
index = my_tuple.index('a')
print(index)
```

It's important to note that these methods do not modify the original tuple but rather provide information about its elements.

Have a look at tuplemethods.py

Sets

Sets are mutable, unordered collections of unique elements. They are useful when you want to store a collection of items without any duplicates. Sets are defined using curly braces {}

```
my_set = {1, 2, 3, 4, 5}
```

Two things to note about sets. Firstly, you can't index individual elements in the set as it is an unordered data type. Secondly, all items must be unique.

Sets are useful when working with collections of unique elements and they allow you to perform operations like eliminating duplicates, set algebra, and efficient membership testing. They are particularly useful in scenarios where you need to keep track of distinct values or perform mathematical operations on sets of elements.

There are several built-in methods that allow you to perform various operations and manipulations on sets. Here are some common ones:

1. **add()** adds an element to the set. If the element is already present, it is not added again.

```
my_set = {1, 2, 3}
my_set.add(4)
```

2. **remove()** removes a specified element from the set. If the element is not found, it raises a `KeyError`.

```
my_set = {1, 2, 3}
my_set.remove(2)
```

3. **discard()** removes a specified element from the set. If the element is not found, it does nothing and does not raise an error.

```
my_set = {1, 2, 3}
my_set.discard(2)
```

4. **pop()** removes and returns an arbitrary element from the set. Since sets are unordered, the popped element may vary.

```
my_set = {1, 2, 3}
popped_element = my_set.pop()
```

5. **clear()** removes all elements from the set, making it empty.

```
my_set = {1, 2, 3}
my_set.clear()
```

6. **union()** returns a new set containing all elements from the current set and another set or iterable.

```
set1 = {1, 2, 3}
set2 = {3, 4, 5}
union_set = set1.union(set2)
```

7. **intersection()** returns a new set containing common elements between the current set and another set or iterable.

```
set1 = {1, 2, 3}
set2 = {3, 4, 5}
intersection_set = set1.intersection(set2)
```

8. **difference()** returns a new set containing elements that are in the current set but not in another set or iterable.

```
set1 = {1, 2, 3}
set2 = {3, 4, 5}
difference_set = set1.difference(set2)
```

9. **symmetric_difference()** returns a new set containing elements that are in either the current set or another set, but not both.

```
set1 = {1, 2, 3}
set2 = {3, 4, 5}
symmetric_diff_set = set1.symmetric_difference(set2)
```

10. **issubset()** checks whether the current set is a subset of another set or iterable. Returns `True` or `False`.

```
set1 = {1, 2}
set2 = {1, 2, 3, 4}
is_subset = set1.issubset(set2)
```

11. **issuperset()** checks whether the current set is a superset of another set or iterable. Returns `True` or `False`.

```
set1 = {1, 2, 3, 4}
set2 = {1, 2}
is_superset = set1.issuperset(set2)
```

Have a look at setmethods.py. Give them a try.

Lab Exercises 3.2

1. Write a Python program that takes two sets and prints the union, intersection, and difference of the two sets.
2. Write a Python program that takes a tuple of integers and prints a new tuple with the following modifications:
   - All even numbers are multiplied by 2.
   - All odd numbers are incremented by 1.
3. Write a Python program that takes a tuple of names and prints the names in alphabetical order.
4. Write a Python program that takes a string and prints a set containing all unique characters in the string.

5. Write a Python program that takes two sets and performs the following operations:
   - Prints the union of the two sets.
   - Prints the intersection of the two sets.
   - Prints the symmetric difference of the two sets.
6. Write a Python program that takes a tuple of numbers as input and calculates the sum and average of the numbers in the tuple. Print both the sum and average.

   For example, given the tuple (10, 20, 30, 40, 50), the program should calculate the sum as 150 and the average as 30.0.

Dictionaries

Dictionaries are key-value pairs used to store and retrieve data efficiently. They are unordered and mutable. Each element in a dictionary is referenced by a key rather than a position.

Dictionaries are defined using curly braces {} and consist of key-value pairs separated by colons.

```
my_dict = {"name": "John",
           "age": 25,
           "city": "New York"}
```

To read a value, put the key in square brackets.

```
my_dict["name"]
```

This will point to name

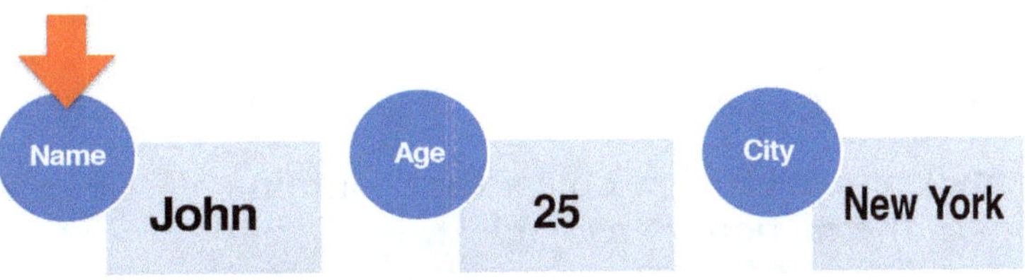

To change or add a value, put the key in square brackets, then assign the value. For example, if we change name 'John' to 'Mike'.

```
my_dict["name"] = "Mike"
```

This will change the data assigned to the 'name' key

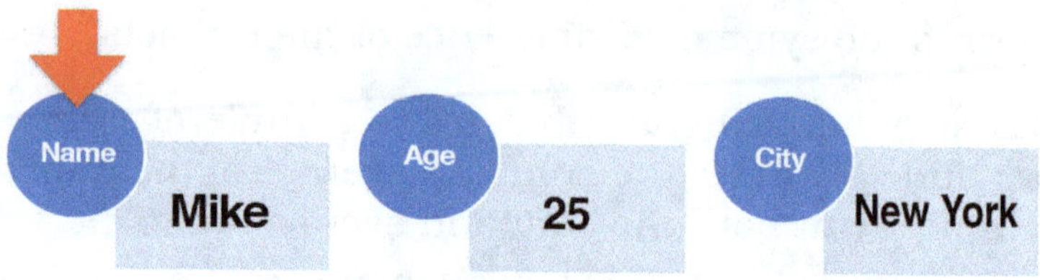

To add an item, use the .update() method. Enclose the data to add in braces {'Key' : 'Data'}. If the key doesn't exist, it will add the item to the end.

```
my_dict.update( {'Country': 'USA'} )
```

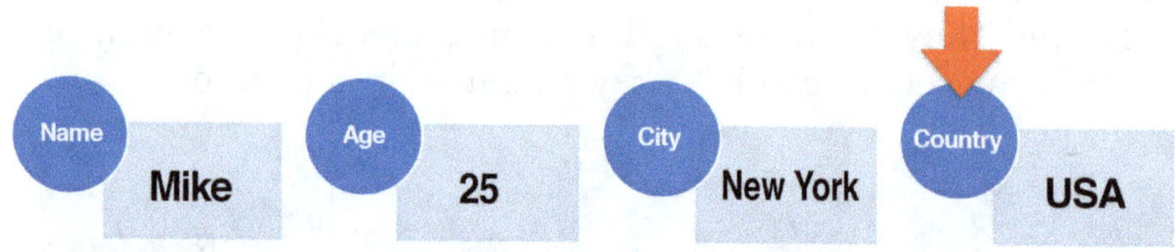

There several built-in methods that allow you to perform various operations on dictionaries. Here are some commonly used methods:

1. **keys()** returns a view object that contains all the keys in the dictionary.

    ```
    my_dict = {"name": "John", "age": 25, "country":
              "USA"}
    keys = my_dict.keys()
    ```

2. **values()** returns a view object that contains all the values in the dictionary.

    ```
    my_dict = {"name": "John", "age": 25, "country":
              "USA"}
    values = my_dict.values()
    ```

3. **items()** returns a view object that contains all the key-value pairs in the dictionary as tuples.

```
my_dict = {"name": "John", "age": 25, "country":
           "USA"}
items = my_dict.items()
```

4. **get()** returns the value for a specified key. If the key is not found, it returns a default value or None.

```
my_dict = {"name": "John", "age": 25, "country":
          "USA"}
age = my_dict.get("age")
```

5. **pop()** removes and returns the value for a specified key. If the key is not found, it raises a `KeyError` or returns a default value.

```
my_dict = {"name": "John", "age": 25, "country":
          "USA"}
age = my_dict.pop("age")
```

6. **popitem()** removes and returns the last inserted key-value pair as a tuple. If the dictionary is empty, it raises a `KeyError`.

```
my_dict = {"name": "John", "age": 25, "country":
          "USA"}
last_item = my_dict.popitem()
```

7. **update()** updates the dictionary with the key-value pairs from another dictionary or an iterable.

```
my_dict = {"name": "John", "age": 25, "country":
          "USA"}
other_dict = {"occupation": "Engineer", "city":
              "New York"}
my_dict.update(other_dict)
```

8. **clear()** removes all key-value pairs from the dictionary, making it empty.

```
my_dict = {"name": "John", "age": 25, "country":
          "USA"}
my_dict.clear()
```

Have a look at dictionarymethods.py.

Study the code to see how the methods work.

Lab Exercises 3.3

1. Write a program that creates a dictionary representing a person's contact information. The dictionary should include keys for 'name', 'email', and 'phone'. Prompt the user to enter values for each key and then print the dictionary.

2. Write a program that simulates a simple English to Spanish dictionary. The program should prompt the user to enter an English word and then print the corresponding Spanish translation. Use a dictionary to store the word translations. For example:

English	Spanish
Hello	Hola
Goodbye	Adiós
Thank you	Gracias
Yes	Sí
No	No
Food	Comida
Water	Agua
Time	Tiempo

3. Write a program that tracks the sales of products in a store. The program should allow the user to enter the name and price of each product sold, and update the sales information accordingly. It should keep a running total of the sales amount for each product. The program should also provide the option to display the total sales amount for each product.

4. How do you merge two dictionaries into one?

5. How do you define a dictionary in Python?

6. How do you access an item in a dictionary?

7. How do you use the get() method to retrieve the value associated with a specific key in a dictionary?

8. How do you use the pop() method to remove a key-value pair from a dictionary and retrieve its value?

9. How do you use the update() method to merge two dictionaries into one?

Summary

- Data structures are used to organize and store data in a structured manner.
- There are several built-in data structures in Python, including
  - lists
  - 2D lists
  - tuples
  - sets
  - dictionaries
- Lists are ordered, mutable, and can contain elements of different data types.
- Lists have built-in methods for manipulation, such as append, extend, insert, remove, pop, index, count, sort, reverse, and copy.
- 2D lists are lists of lists, representing data in a tabular form with rows and columns. Items are accessed using row and column indexes and have methods for manipulation, such as len, indexing, appending, extending, inserting, and popping.
- Tuples are similar to lists but are immutable, meaning their elements cannot be modified.
- Sets are mutable, unordered collections of unique elements.
- Sets have methods for adding, removing, popping, clearing, and performing set operations like union, intersection, difference, symmetric difference, issubset, and issuperset.
- Dictionaries are key-value pairs used to store and retrieve data efficiently.
- Dictionaries are unordered and mutable, and they have methods for accessing keys, values, items, getting values by key, popping values by key, updating with another dictionary, and clearing the dictionary.
- Dictionaries have several built-in methods that allow you to perform various operations.

4 File Handling

File handling is the process of working with files and involves performing various operations such as reading from files, writing to files, and manipulating file data.

When a program terminates or the computer is turned off, data is lost. For this reason, a file provides a means to store data beyond the runtime of a program. In other words, you can store data permanently, so it is available the next time the program runs. Python provides built-in functions and methods for file handling, making it easy to perform these operations. You can open files in different modes, read data from files, write data to files, navigate within files, and handle errors that may occur during file operations.

For this chapter, you'll need to download the source code files from:

`elluminetpress.com/pyf`

You'll also find various video demos and tutorials.

Files are used to store data and you can save structured or unstructured data such as text, numbers, images, audio, and video.

This data is read and displayed or manipulated as needed by the program. Files serve as a common medium for data exchange between systems and applications and can also be used to store configuration settings for applications. Instead of hard-coding configuration values within the program, you can read them from a configuration file. This allows for easy modification of settings without changing the source code.

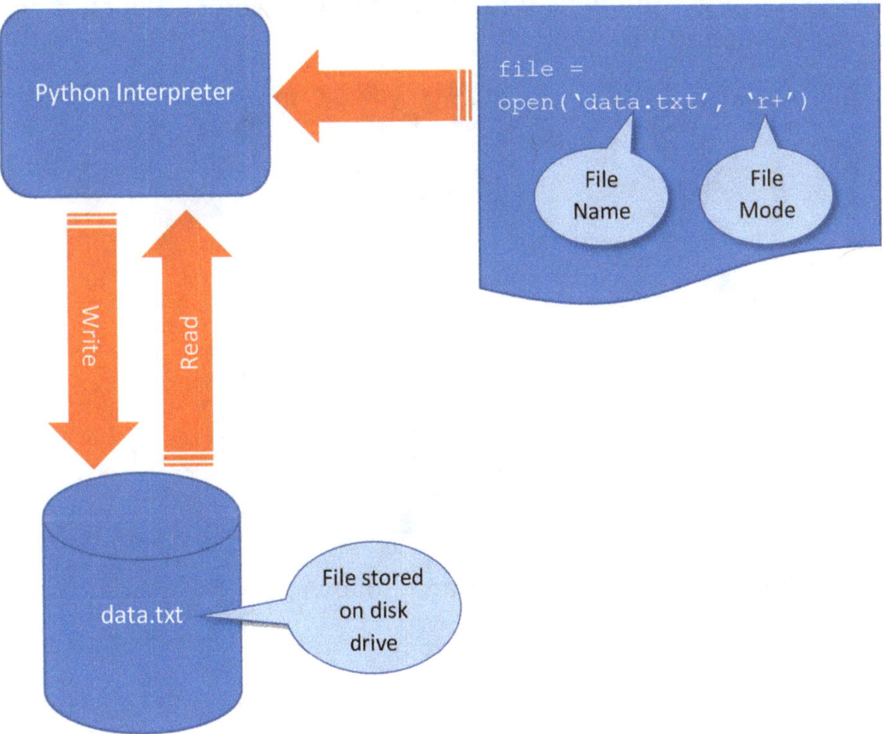

There are two different types of files: text and binary. Text files store data as plain text, typically using a specific character encoding such as ASCII or Unicode. These files contain human readable text and can be opened with a text editor such as notepad. Text files are often used for storing and exchanging textual data, such as plain text documents, source code files, configuration files, and CSV files.

Binary files store data in a binary format, which means they represent data as sequences of binary values (or bytes) as they are stored in memory. Binary files are not directly human-readable as they don't follow a specific character encoding and are often used for storing and exchanging non-textual data, such as multimedia files, databases, executable files, and serialized data.

Opening a File

By default, Python opens a file in text mode. You can open a file using the open() function.

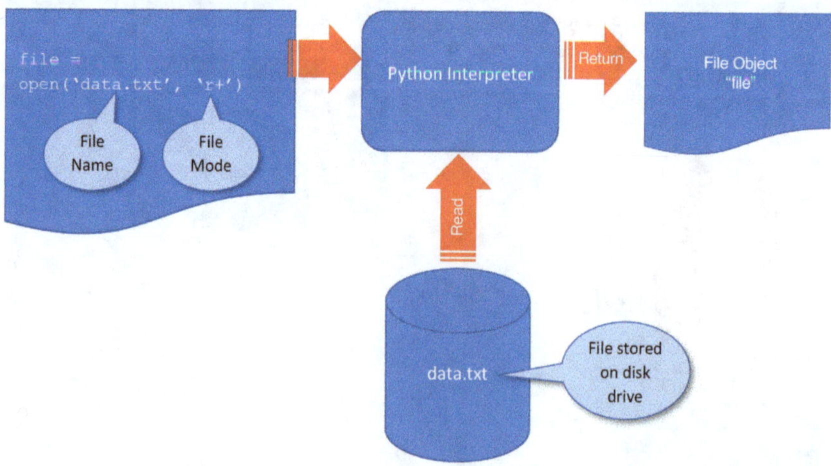

In the parenthesis, list the filename followed by the mode.

```
my_file = open("filename", "mode")
```

The mode specifies how a file should be opened and accessed. Let's take a look at the common modes:

- **"r"** stands for read mode (default) and opens a file for reading only. The file needs to exist.
- **"w"** stands for write mode and opens a file for writing. This mode will create a new file if it doesn't exist or truncates the file if it exists.
- **"a"** stands for append mode and opens the file for appending. Data will be written at the end of the file.

- **"r+"** stands for read and write mode. Opens the file for both reading and writing. The file must exist.
- **"w+"** stands for write and read mode. Similar to "r+", but it truncates the file to zero length if it exists or creates a new file if it doesn't exist.
- **"a+"** stands for append and read mode. Opens the file for both appending and reading. Data written to the file is added at the end, and the file is not truncated. It creates a new file if it doesn't exist.

Once the open() function returns a file object, we can work on the file using the object's methods such as .read() .write() or .close()

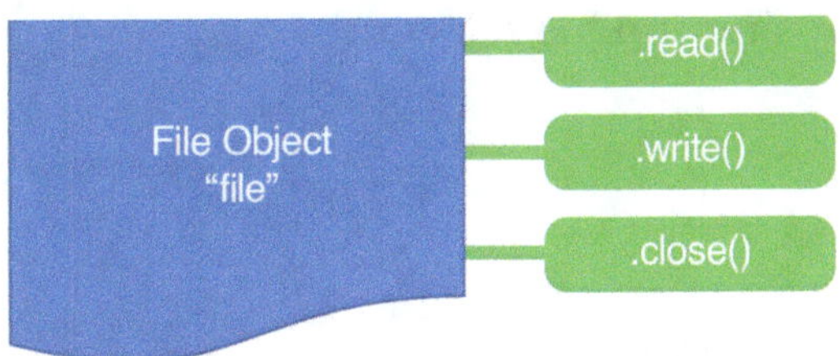

Writing to a File

To write data to a file in Python, you can use the write() or writelines() methods of the file object.

To write some data, first open the file in write mode using the open() function. Specify the file name (eg data.txt), and the mode as `"w"`. This will create a new file or overwrite an existing file.

```
my_file = open("data.txt", "w")
```

With the file open, there are multiple options you can use to write data to a file. You can use the write() method, or the writelines() method. The write() method is used to write a single string or a sequence of characters and allows for more flexibility in writing custom content.

```
my_file.write("This is a sample text.")
```

The writelines() method is convenient when you have a list that you want to write as lines to the file.

This method treats each string as a separate line. If the elements in the list are not already strings, you will need to convert them to strings.

```
lines = ["This is the first line!\n", "This is a sample text.\n"]

my_file.writelines(lines)
```

After writing the data, it's important to close the file using the `close()` method to release system resources and ensure that the data is written to the file.

```
my_file.close()
```

Alternatively, you can use the with statement which automatically takes care of closing the file for you.

```
with open("data.txt", "w") as my_file:
    my_file.write("This is a sample text.\n")
```

Reading Data

To read data from a file you can use the read() or readlines() methods of the file object. To read a file, first open the file in read mode. We'll open the data.txt file we created in the previous section.

```
my_file = open("data.txt", "r")
```

To read the data, there are various options you can use. You can use the read() method if you want to treat the entire content of the file as a single string.

```
content = my_file.read()

print(content)
```

Use the readlines() method to read the contents of the file line by line and store them in a list

```
for line in my_file:

    print(line)
```

After reading the data, it's important to close the file using the `close()` method to release system resources.

```
my_file.close()
```

Alternatively, you can use the with statement, which automatically takes care of closing the file for you.

```
with open("data.txt", "r") as my_file:
    content = my_file.read()
    print(content)
```

Opening a Binary File

You can open a file using the open() function. In the parenthesis, list the filename followed by the mode.

```
my_file = open("filename", "mode")
```

The mode specifies how a file should be opened and accessed. Let's take a look at the common modes:

- **"rb"** stands for read binary mode (default) and opens a file for reading only. The file needs to exist.
- **"wb"** stands for write binary mode and opens a file for writing. This mode will create a new file if it doesn't exist or truncates the file if it exists.
- **"ab"** stands for append binary mode and opens the file for appending. Data will be written at the end of the file.
- **"r+b"** or **"rb+"** stands for read and write binary. This mode allows you to open a binary file for both reading and writing. It provides the capability to read from and write to the file at any position. The file must already exist.
- **"w+b"** or **"wb+"** stands for write and read binary. This mode is similar to "r+b" but creates a new file if it doesn't exist. If the file exists, it will be truncated.
- **"a+b"** or **"ab+"** stands for append and read binary. This mode allows you to open a binary file for both appending data at the end and reading from it. The file will be created if it doesn't exist.

Writing to a Binary File

Writing to binary files in Python involves storing data in a binary format, which is useful for working with non-textual data or when you need to preserve the exact byte representation of the data. First, we need to open the file in write binary mode.

```
my_file = open("data.dat", "wb")
```

To write data to the file, use the write() method of the file object to write data to the file. In binary mode, the write() method expects bytes, so you need to convert your data to bytes before writing it to the file.

You can do this using the bytes() or bytearray() functions. If you have data that should not be modified once created (such as string literals or constant data), use bytes(). If you need to manipulate or modify the data, such as when processing or updating byte sequences, bytearray() provides the necessary mutability.

Here is our data

```
data = "This is a string!"
```

As you can see this is a string, so we need to convert. You can use the bytes() to convert the data to bytes:

```
bytes_data = bytes(data, "utf-8")
```

Or you can use the bytearray(). For example:

```
bytes_data = bytearray(data, "utf-8")
```

With these functions, we can also specify the encoding such as "utf-8". UTF-8 is a widely used character encoding that can represent any Unicode character. It is the default encoding for Python strings and is commonly used for encoding text data.

Now that we have converted the data to bytes, we can write the data to the file using the write() method.

```
my_file.write(bytes_data)
```

Or you can simply prefix the string with b.

```
file.write(b"Hello, World!")
```

Remember to close your file at the end.

```
my_file.close()
```

Reading a Binary File

First we need to open the file in read binary mode. Make sure the file exists first.

```
my_file = open("data.dat", "rb")
```

To read the data, we can use the read() method. The read() method is used to read a specified number of bytes from a file or the entire content if no size is specified. It returns a byte object in binary mode containing the data.

```
content = my_file.read()
print(content)
```

Using the read() method you can also specify the number of bytes to read. The following example will read the first 4 bytes of the file.

```
binary_data = file.read(4)
```

You can also use the readline() method. The readline() method is used to read a single line from a file. It returns a byte object in binary mode representing the line.

```
line = my_file.readline()
print(line)
```

Remember to close your file at the end.

```
my_file.close()
```

Random File Access

When a file is opened, the Python Interpreter allocates a pointer within the file.

This pointer determines the position in the file from where reading or writing will take place. The pointer can be moved to any location in the file.

To move the file pointer, use the .seek() method.

```
file.seek(position-in-file, whence)
```

The first parameter (position-in-file) determines how many bytes to move. A positive value will move the pointer forward, a negative value will move the pointer backward. The position in the file is called an offset.

The second parameter (whence) determines where in the file to start from, and accepts one of three values:

- 0 : sets the start point to the beginning of the file (the default)
- 1 : sets the start point to the current position
- 2 : sets the start point to the end of the file

In a file, each position could contain one byte or one character. Remember, the numbering system starts with 0.

Using our text file as an example file.seek(5) would move the file pointer to the 6th byte.

	0	1	2	3	4	5	6	7	8	9	10	11	12	13	14	15	16	17
	J	a	c	k		j	a	c	k	@	t	e	s	t	.	c	o	m
18	P	e	t	e		p	e	t	e	@	t	e	s	t	.	c	o	m

Use:

```
file.seek(23, 0)
```

This will move the pointer to position 23 from the beginning of the file

	0	1	2	3	4	5	6	7	8	9	10	11	12	13	14	15	16	17
	J	a	c	k		j	a	c	k	@	t	e	s	t	.	c	o	m
18	P	e	t	e		p	e	t	e	@	t	e	s	t	.	c	o	m
36	J	i	l	l		j	i	l	l	@	s	i	t	e	.	c	o	m

If you want to read from the end of the file, you'll need to count backwards from the end of the file, you do this with a negative offset.

The seek() function with negative offset only works when file is opened in binary mode.

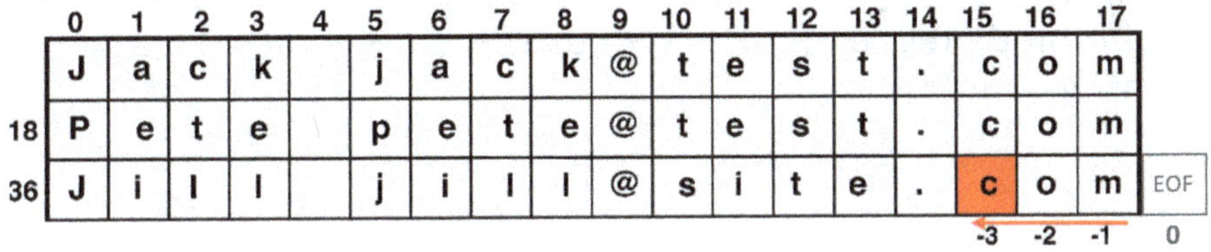

	0	1	2	3	4	5	6	7	8	9	10	11	12	13	14	15	16	17	
	J	a	c	k		j	a	c	k	@	t	e	s	t	.	c	o	m	
18	P	e	t	e		p	e	t	e	@	t	e	s	t	.	c	o	m	
36	J	i	l	l		j	i	l	l	@	s	i	t	e	.	c	o	m	EOF
																-3	-2	-1	0

To move the pointer from the end of the file

```
f.seek(-3, 2)
```

Use .decode('utf-8') to convert the binary back to text.

```
datafromfile = f.readline().decode('utf-8')
```

To find the current position of the file pointer in the file use the .tell() method.

```
file.tell()
```

Let's take a look at a program. Open the file fileseek.py. This file reads data from data.text, moves the pointer to the 6th character and outputs the line to the screen.

```
#open file for reading
file = open ('data.txt' , 'r')

#move pointer to the 6th character in the file
file.seek (5,0)

#read line in file starting from 6th character
dataInFile = file.readline()

print (dataInFile)

#close the file
file.close()
```

This will output the following, as the 6th character is 'j'.

```
jack@test.com
```

You can see that the output will terminate at the end of the line.

File Handling Methods

Here is a summary of methods available for file objects. You can tag the method names below onto the object name using the following syntax:

```
fileobject.method()
```

Here we have various methods to close a file, as well as some other common methods.

Method	Description
close()	Closes the file
detach()	Returns the separated raw stream from the buffer
fileno()	Returns a number that represents the stream, from the operating system's perspective
flush()	Flushes the internal buffer
isatty()	Returns whether the file stream is interactive or not

Next, there are methods to read data from a file. You can read the whole file, or return lines from a file.

Method	Description
read()	Returns the file content
readable()	Returns whether the file stream can be read or not
readline()	Returns one line from the file
readlines()	Returns a list of lines from the file

Various methods to write data to a file. You can check whether a file is writable, or you can write data to a file.

Method	Description
writable()	Returns whether the file can be written to or not
write()	Writes the specified string to the file
writelines()	Writes a list of strings to the file

Various other methods to seek a file position, as well as a method to return the current position in a file and one to truncate the file to a specific size.

Method	Description
`seek()`	Change the file position
`seekable()`	Returns whether the file allows us to change the file position
`tell()`	Returns the current file position
`truncate()`	Resizes the file to a specified size

Data Serialisation

Data serialization is the process of converting data structures or objects into a format that can be easily stored, transmitted, or reconstructed later.

It involves converting the data into a stream of bytes that can be saved to a file or sent over a network.

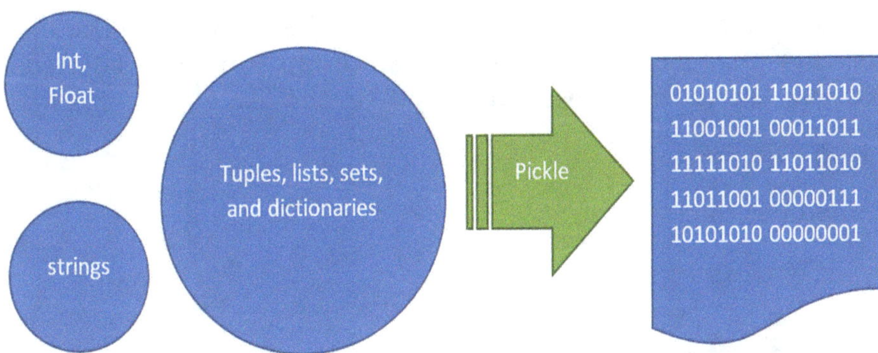

Python provides several built-in modules for data serialization such as pickle and JSON.

Pickle

The pickle module allows you to serialize Python objects into a binary format and deserialize them back into Python objects. Pickle supports a wide range of Python data types and object hierarchies.

Writing Data

Here below are the methods to write/serialize the data.

Method	Description
pickle.dump()	used to serialize and write Python objects to a binary file using the Pickle module.
pickle.dumps()	used to serialize Python objects and return the serialized data as a byte string, without writing it to a file.

First, we need to import the pickle module.

```
import pickle
```

Next, we need to open a file. In this example, we want to write the data to the file, so we open it in write binary mode.

```
my_file = open("pickleddata.dat", "wb")
```

Let's say we want to store the following list in a binary file.

```
data = [1, 2, 3, 4, 5]
```

To do this, we need to serialise the data then write it to the file. For this purpose we use the pickle.dump() function. This will serialise the data and write it directly to the file.

```
pickle.dump(data, my_file)
```

Remember to close your file

```
my_file.close()
```

Reading Data

Here below are some methods to read/deserialize the data read from the file.

Method	Description
pickle.load()	used to deserialize and load Python objects from a binary file that was previously serialized using pickle.dump()
pickle.loads()	used to deserialize and load Python objects from a byte string that was previously serialized using pickle.dumps()

First, we need to import the pickle module.

```
import pickle
```

Next, we need to open a file. In this example, we want to read the data from the file, so we open it in read binary mode.

```
my_file = open("pickleddata.dat", "rb")
```

Now that we have the file open, we want to read the data. We can so this using the pickle.load() function.

```
data = pickle.load(file)
```

Remember to close your file at the end.

```
my_file.close()
```

JSON

The JSON module provides functions for working with JSON (JavaScript Object Notation) data.

It allows you to serialize Python objects into a JSON string and deserialize them back into Python objects.

JSON is a popular format for data interchange between different systems and programming languages, but it supports a limited set of data types, including strings, numbers, booleans, arrays, objects, and null, however it does not have explicit support for complex data types like dates or binary data.

When working with JSON, the file does not need to be in binary format. JSON is a text-based data interchange format, so it can be read from and write to regular text files.

Writing Data

Here below are the methods to write/serialize the data.

Method	Description
json.dump ()	used to serialize and write Python objects as JSON data to a file.
json.dumps ()	used to serialize Python objects as JSON-formatted strings.

First, we need to import the JSON module.

```
import json
```

Next, we need to open a file. In this example, we want to write the data to the file, so we open it in write mode.

```
my_file = open("jsonddata.dat", "w")
```

Let's say we want to store the following dictionary in a file.

```
my_data = {
    'name': 'Sam',
    'age': 32,
    'city': 'Seattle'
}
```

Use the json.dump() function to convert the data then write it to the file. Pass the data object and the file object as an argument.

```
json.dump(my_data, my_file)
```

Remember to close your file at the end.

```
my_file.close()
```

Reading Data

Here are the methods to read/deserialize the data.

Method	Description
json.load ()	used to deserialize and load JSON data from a file or a file-like object.
json.loads ()	used to deserialize and load JSON-formatted strings into Python objects

First, we need to import the JSON module.

```
import json
```

Next, we need to open a file. In this example, we want to read the data from the file, so we open it in read mode.

```
my_file = open("jsonddata.dat", "r")
```

We use the json.load() function to read the data from the file and convert it back to a Python dictionary.

```
json_data = json.load(my_file)
```

Remember to close your file at the end.

```
my_file.close()
```

Error Handling

When working with files, it's important to handle potential errors that may occur during file operations. Common errors include file not found, permission denied, or disk full. You can use try-except blocks to catch and handle these errors gracefully. See page 107 for more information on error & exception handling.

```
try:
    file_path = "my_file.txt"
    file = open(file_path, "r")
    content = file.read()
    print("File content:", content)
    file.close()

except FileNotFoundError:
    print(f"File '{file_path}' not found!")

except PermissionError:
    print(f"Permission denied '{file_path}'!")

except IOError as e:
   print(f"I/O error occurred '{file_path}':", str(e))

except Exception as e:
    print("An error occurred:", str(e))
```

In this example, we attempt to open a file named "my_file.txt" for reading. However, if the file is not found, a FileNotFoundError will be raised.

If the file access is denied due to permissions, a PermissionError will be raised. Any other I/O-related errors will be caught by the IOError block. Finally, any other unexpected exceptions will be caught by the Exception block.

Lab Exercises 4.1

1. What is file handling in Python, and what are its key components?
2. How do files provide permanent storage for data in Python programs?
3. What built-in functions and methods does Python provide for file handling?
4. What are the two types of files in Python, and what is the difference between them?
5. How can you open a file in Python? Show examples.
6. What are some common modes used when opening a file in Python?
7. How can you write data to a file in Python? Show an example
8. Why is it important to close a file after writing data to it?
9. How can you read data from a file in Python? Show an example.
10. Why is it important to close a file after reading data from it?
11. How can you handle binary files in Python? Are there any differences compared to text files?
12. What is the process of writing data to a binary file? How can data be converted to bytes?
13. How can you read data from a binary file in Python? Show an example
14. What is data serialization, and why is it useful?
15. How can the pickle module be used for serialization and deserialization of Python objects? Show examples
16. What functionality does the JSON module provide for working with JSON data in Python? Show examples.
17. How can the pickle module be used for file handling with serialization?
18. How can the JSON module be used for file handling with JSON data?

Summary

- File handling involves working with files, including reading, writing, and manipulating file data.
- Files allow data to be stored beyond the runtime of a program, providing permanent storage for future program runs.
- Python provides built-in functions and methods for file handling, making it easy to perform file operations.
- Files can store structured or unstructured data such as text, numbers, images, audio, and video.
- There are two types of files: text files (human-readable) and binary files (non-human-readable).
- Opening a file in Python is done using the open() function, specifying the filename and mode.
- Common modes include read, write, append, read and write, write and read, and append and read.
- Writing data to a file can be done using the write() or writelines() methods of the file object.
- Closing the file after writing is important to release system resources and ensure data is written.
- Reading data from a file can be done using the read() or readlines() methods of the file object.
- Closing the file after reading is important to release system resources.
- Binary files can be opened and written/read using similar modes as text files, but with “b” appended.
- Writing to a binary file involves converting data to bytes using bytes() or bytearray() functions.
- Reading a binary file involves using the read() or readline() methods to retrieve binary data.
- Data serialization is the process of converting data into a format for storage or transmission. Use pickle or JSON.

5

Python Functions

A function is a block of reusable code that performs a specific task and allows you to divide your program into smaller, modular pieces, making it easier to read, understand, and maintain. Functions also help in code reusability and promote a more organized and efficient programming approach.

Python provides a vast library of built-in functions that perform common operations. These functions are available and read for use. Some examples include

- print()
- input()
- len()
- max()
- min()
- sum()

You can also define your own functions.

For this chapter, you'll need to download the source code files from:

`elluminetpress.com/pyfns`

You'll also find various video demos and tutorials.

For example, the function addNum shown below in figure 1 takes two numbers, adds them together, and returns the result.

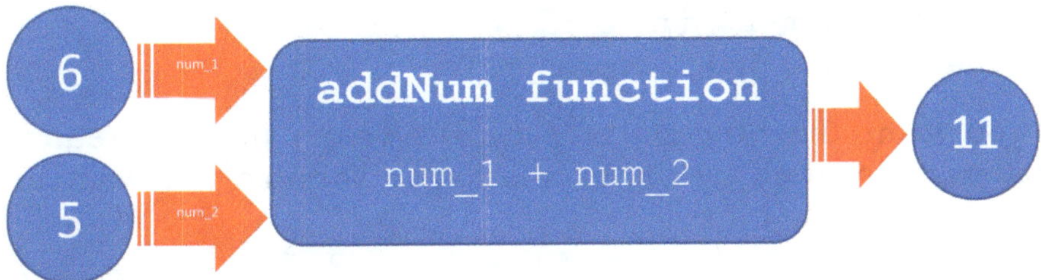

The terms "arguments" and "parameters" are often used interchangeably, but they are not the same thing.

Parameters are the variables defined in a function's declaration or definition. They act as placeholders for the values that will be passed to the function when it is called. Parameters are specified within the parentheses after the function name.

```
def addNum (num_1, num_2):
```

Arguments are the actual values passed to a function when it's called. They correspond to the parameters defined in the function's definition. Arguments are provided within the parentheses when calling a function.

```
num_1 = 10
num_2 = 20
addNum (num_1, num_2)
```

Declaring Functions

You can declare functions using the def keyword followed by the function name, parentheses, and a colon. Choose a descriptive name that reflects the purpose or action performed by the function. Make sure the name you choose isn't already used as a built-in function name or keyword.

```
def function_name(parameters):
    # Function body
    # Statements to be executed when function called
    # Return a value using the return statement
```

For example. Add any parameters the function takes inside the parentheses.

```
def addNum(num_1, num_2):
    return num_1 + num_2
```

If you want the function to return a value, use the return statement followed by the expression or variable you want to return.

Calling Functions

To call a function, use the function name followed by parentheses. Within the parentheses, provide any necessary arguments or leave them empty if the function doesn't require any.

For example, to call the addNum() function we defined above

```
result = addNum(4, 4)
```

This is what happens when we call the function. Arguments 4 & 4 are passed to the function.

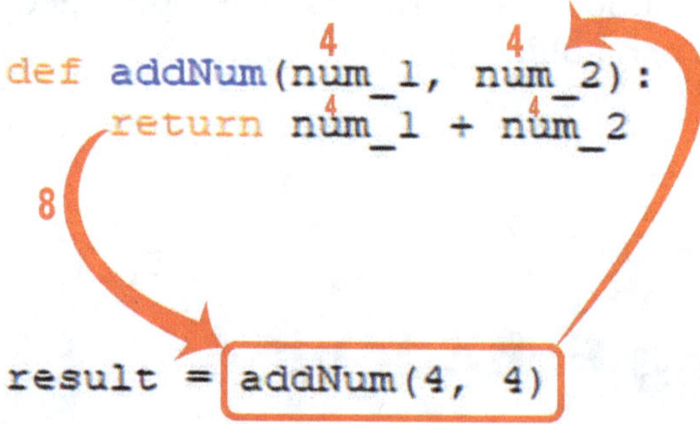

The function adds these together then returns the result to the function call.

Lab Exercise 5.1

1. Write a Python function called "calculate_average" that takes a list of numbers as a parameter and calculates the average of those numbers. The function should return the average as the result.

Function Argument Types

Function arguments are the values or variables that are passed to a function when it is called. They allow you to provide input to the function and perform operations based on that input. In Python, there are different types of function arguments.

Positional Arguments

Positional Arguments are the most common type of arguments and are passed based on their position in the function call. The order and number of arguments must match the function definition. For example.

```
def greet(name, age):
    print(f"Hello {name}, you are {age} years old.")

greet("Alice", 25)
```

In this example, the greet function takes two positional arguments: name and age. When we call the function greet("Alice", 25), the value "Alice" is assigned to the name parameter and 25 is assigned to the age parameter. The function then prints the greeting message using the provided values: Hello Alice, you are 25 years old.

Default Arguments

Default Arguments have predefined values that are used if no argument value is provided in the function call. They are specified in the function definition by assigning a default value to the corresponding parameter. For example

```
def greet(name, age=30):
    print(f"Hello {name}, you are {age} years old.")

greet("Alice")
greet("Bob", 40)
```

In this example, the greet function has a default argument age=30. If the age argument is not provided when calling the function, it will default to 30.

When we call greet("Alice"), only the name argument is passed, and since we haven't provided the age argument, it takes the default value of 30.

The output will be: Hello Alice, you are 30 years old. When we call greet("Bob", 40), both the name and age arguments are passed explicitly, overriding the default value. The output will be: Hello Bob, you are 40 years old.

Using default arguments allows us to provide a default value for a parameter if the caller doesn't provide a value for it

Keyword Arguments

Keyword Arguments are passed using the name of the parameter followed by the argument value.

```
name="Alice", age=25, city="New York")
```

This allows you to specify arguments out of order and is particularly useful when dealing with functions that have many parameters or when you want to make the code more readable.

```
def describe_person(name, age, city):
    print(f"{name} is {age} years old and lives in
          {city}.")

describe_person(name="Alice", age=25, city="New
               York")

describe_person(age=30, name="Bob", city="London")
```

In this example, the describe_person function has three parameters: name, age, and city. When calling the function, we use keyword arguments to specify the values for each parameter. The order of the keyword arguments doesn't matter as long as we specify the parameter names. In the first call to describe_person, we provide the values for name, age, and city using keyword arguments. The output will be:

```
Alice is 25 years old and lives in New York.
```

In the second call to describe_person, we rearrange the order of the keyword arguments, but still provide values for all three parameters.

The output will be:

```
Bob is 30 years old and lives in London.
```

Using keyword arguments allows us to provide values for specific parameters without relying on the order of the arguments. It makes the function call more explicit and self-explanatory, especially when there are many parameters or when the order of the parameters can be ambiguous.

Variable Length

Variable-Length Arguments allows you to define functions that can accept different numbers of arguments. There are two types of variable-length arguments:

Using *args allows a function to accept any number of positional arguments. The arguments are packed into a tuple, which can be iterated over within the function. For example

```
def calculate_sum(*args):
    total = 0
    for num in args:
        total += num
    return total
```

In this example, the calculate_sum function can accept a different number of arguments. In other words, any number of arguments can be passed to the function and are stored in a tuple called args.

Inside the function, we iterate over the args tuple and calculate the sum of all the values. The total variable is initialized as 0 and then incremented by each value in the args tuple.

When calling calculate_sum, we can provide any number of arguments separated by commas. The function will collect all the arguments and put them into a tuple called args. In each function call, the sum of the arguments will be calculated and returned.

```
print(calculate_sum(1, 2, 3))
print(calculate_sum(10, 20, 30, 40, 50))
print(calculate_sum(2, 4, 6, 8, 10, 12, 14))
```

Using **kwargs allows a function to acccpt any number of keyword arguments. The arguments are packed into a dictionary, which can be accessed by the keys within the function.

```
def print_details(**kwargs):
    for key, value in kwargs.items():
        print(f"{key}: {value}")
```

In this example, the print_details function can accept a different number of keyword arguments – in other words any number of keyword arguments can be passed to the function and are stored in a dictionary called kwargs.

Inside the function, we iterate over the key-value pairs of the kwargs dictionary using the items() method. We then print each key-value pair in the desired format.

When calling the function, we can provide any number of keyword arguments where each keyword argument is specified as key=value.

```
print_details(name="Alice", age=25)
print_details(name="Bob", occupation="Engineer",
             city="New York")
print_details(country="Canada")
```

The function correctly handles all the keyword arguments and prints the details accordingly.

Lab Exercise 5.2

Write a Python function called "calculate_bill" that calculates the total bill amount based on the following parameters:

The base price of the item:

base_price = 100

The tax rate to be applied to the base price

tax_rate = 0.08

The discount percentage to be applied to the base price

discount_percentage = 0.2

Function Scope

Scope refers to the visibility and accessibility of variables, and functions in a particular part of your code. In Python, variables and other identifiers have different levels of scope, which determine where they can be accessed and used.

Variables defined in the global scope are accessible from anywhere in the code, including inside functions (and classes). They are typically declared outside of any function.

```
global_variable = 10

def my_function():
    local_variable = 20
    print(global_variable)
    print(local_variable)

my_function()
print(global_variable)
print(local_variable)
```

Variables defined inside a function have local scope. They are only accessible within that function and nowhere else.

```
global_variable = 10

def my_function():
    local_variable = 20
    print(global_variable)
    print(local_variable)

my_function()
print(global_variable)
print(local_variable) X
```

Once the function execution completes, the variables are destroyed, and their values are no longer accessible. Any result will need to be returned.

Decorator Functions

A decorator function is a higher-order function that takes another function as input and extends or modifies its behavior without directly modifying the function itself. Decorators allow you to wrap or decorate a function with additional functionality, without permanently modifying it.

Decorators are declared using the @ symbol followed by the decorator function name. When the decorated function is called, it can perform actions before and/or after executing the original function.

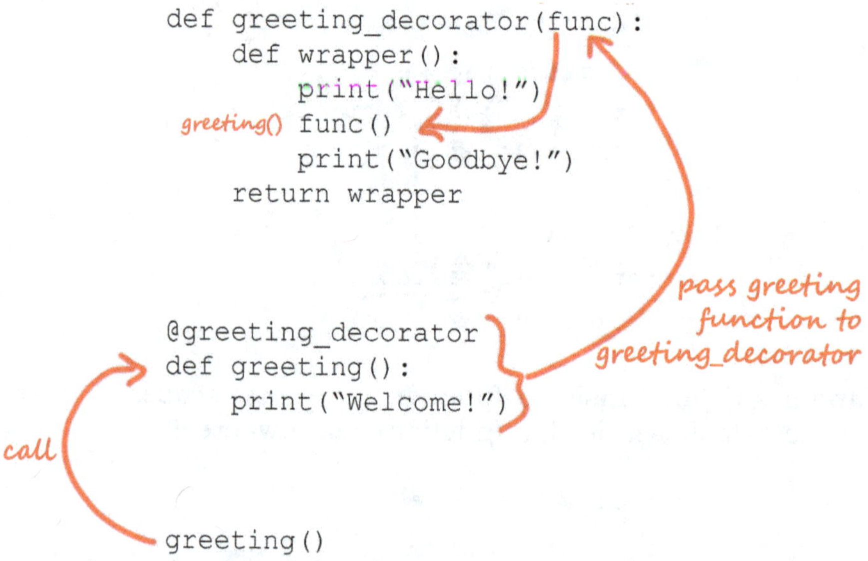

In this example, the greeting_decorator() function is a decorator that adds a greeting message before and after executing the greeting() function. The wrapper() function is the inner function of the decorator that performs the additional actions. It prints "Hello!", then calls the decorated function func() - which is the greeting() function that was passed as an argument to greeting_decorator(). Finally the function prints "Goodbye".

The @greeting_decorator line applies the decorator to the greeting function. So when greeting() is called, it executes the wrapper function defined in the decorator, resulting in the greeting messages being printed around the original "Welcome" message.

Lambda Functions

A lambda function, also known as an anonymous function, is a small and concise function that is defined without a name. It is a way to create a function on-the-fly without the need to define a formal function using the def keyword.

```
lambda arguments: expression
```

Lambda functions are typically used when you need a simple function for a short period of time, often as an argument to higher-order functions or in cases where a named function would be cumbersome.

```
addition = lambda x, y: x + y

result = addition(3, 5)
print(result)
```

In this example, we define a lambda function addition that takes two arguments x and y and returns their sum. We then invoke the lambda function by passing 3 and 5 as arguments, and the result is assigned to the result variable.

```
numbers = [1, 2, 3, 4, 5, 6, 7, 8, 9, 10]

even_numbers = filter(lambda x: x % 2 == 0, numbers)

list_of_numbers = list(even_numbers)

print(list_of_numbers)
```

In this example, we have a list of numbers. We want to filter out the even numbers from the list.

To do this, we use the filter() function and provide a lambda function as the filtering criteria.

The lambda function lambda x: x % 2 == 0 takes each number x and checks if it is divisible by 2 with a remainder of 0. If the condition is true, the number is considered even and is included in the result.

The list() function is used to convert the iterator returned by filter() into a list.

Recursive Functions

A recursive function is a function that calls itself, enabling the function to repeat itself several times.

Recursive programs can also be written using iteration, so why bother with recursion? Well, recursive programs allow programmers to write efficient programs using a minimal amount of code. It's a powerful programming technique that allows a function to solve a problem by breaking it down into smaller sub problems.

Recursion works well for algorithms such as traversing a binary tree, or a sort algorithm and generating fractals. However, if performance is vital, it is better to use iteration, as recursion can be a lot slower.

There are various key components of a recursive function:

- Base Case is the condition that defines the stopping point for the recursion. When the base case is met, the function stops calling itself and returns a value or performs a specific action.
- Recursive Case is the part of the function that calls itself with a modified input. The recursive case reduces the problem size and moves closer to the base case.
- Recursive Function Call is inside the function body, a recursive function calls itself with a different set of arguments. This leads to repeated execution of the function until the base case is reached.

In the example below we have a recursive function that calculates the factorial of a number. Remember, to calculate the factorial you multiply all the numbers from 1 to the given number.

```
def factorial(n):
    if n <= 1:
        return 1
    else:
        return n * factorial(n-1)
```

The function factorial(n) takes an integer n as an argument.

The first if statement checks if n is less than or equal to 1. If n is indeed 1 or less, the function immediately returns 1. This is the base case that terminates the recursion. If the base case is not met (i.e., n is greater than 1), the function executes the else block.

In the else block, the variable a is assigned the value of n multiplied by the result of calling factorial(n-1). This is the recursive case, as the function calls itself with a smaller value (n-1).

The function then returns the value of a, which represents the factorial of n.

When we call the factorial function and pass a positive integer, it will recursively call itself by decreasing the number by one each time: factorial(n-1). Let's take a look at how this works.

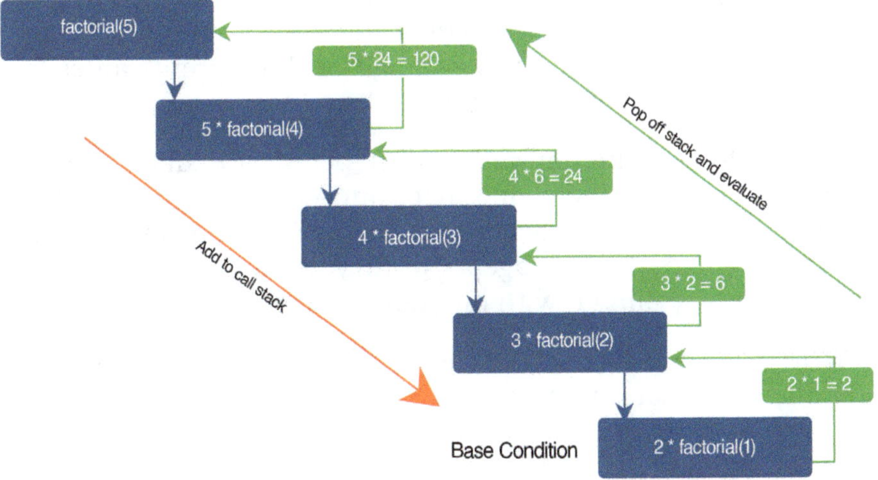

If we call factorial(5)

1. The function checks if the given value n is less than or equal to 1. Since 5 is greater than 1, the else block is executed.

2. Inside the else block, we make a recursive call to factorial(n-1), where n is now 4. This recursive call adds a new instance of the function on the call stack.

3. The process repeats for the recursive calls, and the value of n is decremented each time until it reaches 1.

4. When n becomes 1, the base condition is met, and the function immediately returns 1 without making any further recursive calls.

5. The recursive calls start returning their values one by one, propagating the values back up the call stack.

6. Each recursive call multiplies its respective n value with the returned value from the previous recursive call.

7. Finally, the original call to factorial(5) receives the calculated value, and it is returned resulting in an output of 120. So the factorial of 5, is 5 * 4 * 3 * 2 * 1 which equals 120.

Lab Exercises 5.3

1. Write a Python function called calculate_power that takes in two arguments, base and exponent. If no exponent is provided, the function should calculate the square of the base. Test your function by calling it with different values for base and exponent. Print the results.

2. Write a Python function called print_person_details that takes in three arguments: name, age, and country. The function should print the person's details in the following format: "Name: [name], Age: [age], Country: [country]". Test your function by calling it with different values for the arguments.

3. Write a recursive function called fibonacci() that prints a list of the fibonacci numbers.

   0, 1, 1, 2, 3, 5, 8, 13, 21, 34, 55 and so on.

   Each number is equal to the sum of the preceding two numbers.

4. What's the difference between a parameter and an argument?

5. What is a built in function?

6. What is a user defined function?

7. What makes a function recursive?

8. What is the difference between a local and a global variable?

Summary

- Functions in Python are blocks of reusable code that perform specific tasks, promoting code organization and reusability.
- Python has built-in functions like print(), input(), len(), max(), min(), sum(), range(), and round() that can be readily used.
- User-defined functions can be created using the def keyword, followed by the function name, parentheses, and a colon.
- Parameters are variables defined in a function's declaration, while arguments are the actual values passed to a function when called.
- To call a function, use the function name followed by parentheses, providing necessary arguments.
- Python supports different types of function arguments:
    - Positional arguments are passed based on their position in the function call.
    - Default arguments have predefined values if no argument is provided.
    - Keyword arguments are passed using the parameter name followed by the argument value.
    - Variable-length arguments include *args (for positional arguments) and **kwargs (for keyword arguments).
- Scope determines the visibility and accessibility of variables, with global scope accessible anywhere and local scope limited to a function.
- Recursive functions call themselves, allowing for efficient problem-solving by breaking down tasks into smaller subproblems.
- Recursive functions have a base case (stopping condition) and a recursive case (calling itself with modified input).
- Recursion can be slower than iteration for performance-intensive tasks.
- A factorial function example demonstrates recursion, with a base condition of n <= 1 and recursive case of n * factorial(n-1).

6

Exception Handling

Exception handling is a mechanism that allows you to handle and manage errors or exceptional situations that may occur during the execution of your program. It helps to gracefully handle errors and prevent your program from crashing.

This allows you to handle specific errors gracefully, perform alternative actions, log error messages, and ensure the smooth execution of your program even when unexpected situations occur.

For this chapter, you'll need to download the source code files from:

`elluminetpress.com/pyexc`

You'll also find various video demos and tutorials.

Exception handling is useful in various scenarios. Let's take a look at some common ones.

Input validation. When accepting user input, you can use exception handling to validate and handle any invalid or unexpected input.

File operations. When reading from or writing to files, exception handling is used to handle errors related to file availability, permissions, or unexpected file content.

Network operations. Exception handling is useful when working with network connections. It handles errors related to network connectivity, timeouts, or invalid responses.

Database interactions. When performing database operations, exception handling is crucial to catch and handle errors related to connection failures, query execution, or data integrity issues.

Mathematical operations. When performing calculations or mathematical operations, exception handling can be used to handle errors like division by zero or invalid mathematical operations.

External API integrations. Exception handling is important when integrating with external APIs. It allows you to handle errors related to authentication, rate limits, malformed requests, or unexpected responses.

Handling an Exception

Python uses a try-except block to implement exception handling. The try block is used to enclose the code that may potentially raise an exception, and the except block is used to catch and handle the raised exception.

```
try:
    # Code that may raise an exception

except ExceptionType:
    # Code to handle the exception

finally:
    # Code that always executes
```

In the except block, you state the exception type you are testing for. Substitute ExceptionType with the name of the exception you're testing for. You'll find some common ones in the table on page 108.

The code within the finally block is executed regardless of whether an exception occurred or not. It is commonly used to perform cleanup actions or release resources.

In the table below you'll find some common exceptions.

Exception Type	Description
Exception	Base class for all exceptions in Python.
ValueError	Raised when a function receives an argument of the right type but an inappropriate value.
TypeError	Raised when an operation or function is applied to an object of inappropriate type.
NameError	Raised when a local or global name is not found.
IndexError	Raised when a sequence subscript is out of range.
KeyError	Raised when a dictionary key is not found.
FileNotFoundError	Raised when a file or directory is requested but cannot be found.
PermissionError	Raised when an operation is not permitted.
SyntaxError	Raised when there is a syntax error in the code.
AttributeError	Raised when an attribute reference or assignment fails.
ZeroDivisionError	Raised when division or modulo operation is performed with zero as the denominator.
OverflowError	Raised when a calculation exceeds the maximum limit for a numeric type.
IOError	Raised when an I/O operation fails.
ImportError	Raised when an import statement fails to find the module.

For example, if we wrote a program to get two numbers from the user, then perform a division operation on two numbers entered.

```
num1 = int(input("Enter a number: "))
num2 = int(input("Enter another number: "))
result = num1 / num2
print("The result is:", result)
```

This example could potentially throw up a value error if the user enters a letter instead of a number.

This code could also throw up a divide by zero error if the user enters 0, or an invalid input, if the user enters a non-numeric value.

To prevent the program from crashing, we use exception handling to catch these potential errors.

We can add this code to the try block.

```
try:
    num1 = int(input("Enter a number: "))
    num2 = int(input("Enter another number: "))
    result = num1 / num2
    print("The result is:", result)
```

To tell the interpreter what to do with these errors, we use the except block. The except blocks catch specific exception types (in this case ValueError and ZeroDivisionError) and contains code to handle these errors accordingly. We can find the exception types from table on page 108.

So in our example, we want to display an error message when the user enters a non numeric value, this is a ValueError exception.

```
except ValueError:
    print("Invalid input. Please enter a number.")
```

We also want to display a message if the user enters 0. This is a ZeroDivisionError exception.

```
except ZeroDivisionError:
    print("Cannot divide by zero.")
```

By using exception handling, we can anticipate and handle potential errors, ensuring that our program doesn't crash and providing appropriate feedback to the user when something goes wrong.

By incorporating these techniques into your error handling strategy, you can improve the robustness, reliability, and user-friendliness of your program.

Lab Exercise 6.1

Write a program that calculates the area of a rectangle. The program should prompt the user to enter the length and width of the rectangle. However, the program should handle potential errors that can occur during user input. Add except blocks to handle specific exceptions that may occur during user input:

If the user enters a non-numeric value for length or width.

If the user enters a negative value for length or width.

If any other exception occurs, catch it using the Exception type and display an error message.

Custom Exceptions

A custom exception is one that you define yourself to handle specific types of errors or exceptional situations in your code. By creating custom exceptions, you can provide more descriptive error messages and handle specific cases in a way that aligns with the requirements of your application.

To create a custom exception, you need to define a new class that inherits from one of the built-in exception classes (or types as shown in table 1) provided by Python. For example, ValueError or TypeError. This custom exception class can include additional attributes or methods specific to your needs.

```
class CustomException(ExceptionType):
    pass
```

In the example below, we define a custom exception class called NegativeNumberError by inheriting from the built-in Exception class (see table 1). The pass statement indicates that we're not adding any additional functionality to the exception class.

```
class NegativeNumberError(Exception):
    pass
```

Next, we define a function called square_root that takes a number from the user as input and calculates its square root. If the number is negative, we raise an instance of our custom exception class with a specific error message. Otherwise, we calculate and return the square root.

```
def square_root(number):
    if number < 0:
            raise NegativeNumberError("Cannot use a negative number.")
    else:
        return number ** 0.5
```

In the try block, we prompt the user to enter a number and call the square_root function with the entered number.

If a NegativeNumberError is raised within the function, the corresponding except block is executed, and the custom error message is displayed.

```
try:
    num = float(input("Enter a number: "))
    result = square_root(num)
    print("Square root:", result)
except NegativeNumberError as e:
    print("Error:", str(e))
```

Using custom exceptions allows you to create a more expressive and structured error-handling mechanism in your code, making it easier to handle specific cases and communicate errors effectively.

Let's look at another example. Here, we define a custom exception class called InvalidInputError. This class inherits from the base Exception class. The InvalidInputError class has an __init__ method that accepts a message parameter and assigns it to the instance variable self.message.

```
class InvalidInputError(Exception):
    def __init__(self, message):
        self.message = message
```

We define a function called calculate_factorial that takes a single parameter n. Inside the function, we perform input validation to ensure that n is a non-negative integer. If the input is invalid, we raise an instance of the InvalidInputError exception with an appropriate error message.

The calculate_factorial function then calculates the factorial of n using a for loop and returns the result.

```
def calculate_factorial(n):
    if not isinstance(n, int) or n < 0:
       raise InvalidInputError("Enter positive int")
    result = 1
    for i in range(1, n + 1):
        result *= i
    return result
```

In the try block shown below, we prompt the user to enter a value using the input function and convert it to an integer using the int function. This value is assigned to the variable num. We then call the calculate_factorial function with num as an argument, then assign the returned result to the variable result. If no exceptions occur, we print the factorial of the input number.

```
try:
    num = int(input("Enter positive integer: "))
    result = calculate_factorial(num)
    print("Factorial:", result)
except InvalidInputError as e:
    print("Error:", e.message)
```

If an InvalidInputError exception is raised within the try block, it is caught by the except block. The exception object is assigned to the variable e. We then print an error message along with the message attribute of the exception using e.message.

Lab Exercises 6.2

1. What is exception handling and why is it important in programming?
2. What are some common use cases for exception handling?
3. How is exception handling implemented in Python?
4. What is the purpose of the try block in exception handling?
5. How can you catch and handle specific exceptions using the except block?

6. Write a program that accepts a number from the user and calculates its square. Implement exception handling to handle invalid input. If the user enters a non-numeric value, display an error message and ask for input again until a valid number is entered. Once a valid number is entered, calculate and print its square.
7. Write a program that reads data from a file. Implement exception handling to handle potential errors such as file not found, permission issues, or unexpected file content. If an error occurs, display an appropriate error message. If the file is successfully read, process the data as required.

Summary

- Exception handling allows for the graceful handling of errors and exceptional situations in a program.
- It helps prevent program crashes and enables alternative actions to be taken when unexpected situations occur.
- Common uses of exception handling include input validation, file operations, network operations, database interactions, mathematical operations, and external API integrations.
- Python uses the try-except block to implement exception handling.
- The try block encloses the code that may raise an exception, while the except block catches and handles the raised exception.
- Different exception types can be caught and handled using specific except blocks.
- Custom exceptions can be defined by creating a new class that inherits from one of the built-in exception classes in Python.
- Custom exceptions provide more descriptive error messages and allow for handling specific cases in a tailored way.
- Custom exceptions are raised using the raise statement and can be caught and handled using an appropriate except block.
- Using custom exceptions enhances the error-handling mechanism and improves code structure and communication of errors.

7 Object Oriented Programming

Python is a versatile object-oriented programming language (OOP). Object oriented programming revolves around the concept of objects interacting with each other to model real-world scenarios rather than relying on functions and logic. This makes it well-suited for developing complex applications, building modular code, and creating reusable software components. So understanding OOP principles in Python is vital to enhance code organization, maintainability, and scalability.

Python provides the necessary syntax to define classes, create objects, and implement concepts such as inheritance, encapsulation, polymorphism, and abstraction.

For this chapter, you'll need to download the source code files from:

`elluminetpress.com/pyoo`

You'll also find various video demos and tutorials.

A class is a blueprint for creating objects. It defines the attributes (data) and methods (behaviors) that the objects of that class will use. Classes are defined using the class keyword.

An object is an instance of a class. It represents a specific entity with its own unique set of data and methods (behavior).

Attributes are variables that hold data associated with an object. They are defined within the class and can be accessed and modified using dot notation: object.attribute. Python also supports instance attributes and class attributes.

Methods are functions defined within a class that perform specific actions or operations on the object's data. They are associated with the class and can be called using dot notation object.method().

When creating classes, defining its attributes and methods, you should keep in mind the principles of object-oriented programming.

Encapsulation is the process of bundling data (attributes) and methods (behaviors) that operate on the data within a single unit called a class. It allows for data hiding and provides a clear interface for interacting with the class's objects. Python uses naming conventions to indicate the visibility of attributes and methods.

Inheritance is a key concept in object-oriented programming that allows a class to inherit attributes and methods from another class. A child class inherits attributes and methods from a parent class. The child class is also sometimes called a sub class or derived class, and the parent class is sometimes called the base class or super class.

Polymorphism is the ability of an object to take on different forms or have multiple types and allows objects of different classes to be treated as objects of a common parent. Polymorphism is achieved through inheritance and method overriding, allowing for the implementation of specialized behavior in child classes.

Abstraction involves simplifying complex systems by breaking them down into more manageable and understandable components. It focuses on the essential characteristics of an object or concept while hiding unnecessary details.

Classes & Objects

A class is a blueprint for creating objects. It defines the attributes (data) and methods (behaviors) that the objects of that class will use.

Defining a Class

To define a class, you use the class keyword followed by the class name.

```
class MyClass:
    # Class attributes and methods go here
```

For example, here we've defined a class called Person with attributes and methods.

First, we create a new class named "Person".

```
class Person:
```

Adding Attributes

Next, we define the attributes the class will use. To do this, we use the __init__() method. This is a special method called a constructor and is executed automatically when a new object of the class is created.

```
    def __init__(self, name, age):
        self.name = name
        self.age = age
```

The self parameter refers to the instance of the class being created. It allows you to access and modify the object's attributes. The name and age parameters are used to initialize the name and age attributes of the object. These values are passed as arguments when the object is created and will be assigned to these attributes.

Adding Methods

Next, we define all the methods. The display_info() method is defined within the class.

It takes the self parameter, which allows the method to access the attributes of the object. This method prints the values of the name and age attributes.

```
def display_info(self):
    print(f"Name: {self.name}")
    print(f"Age: {self.age}")
```

Creating & Using Objects

You can create an object of a class by calling the class name followed by parentheses. This returns a new object with its own set of attributes.

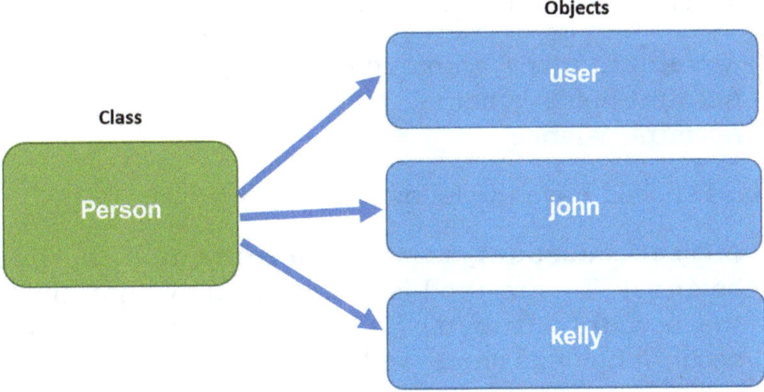

For example, lets create an object and pass some data to it.

```
user = Person("Alice", 25)
```

This creates an object (user) of the Person class. The arguments "Alice" and "25" are assigned to the object's attributes name and age.

```
class Person:
    def __init__(self, name, age):
        self.name = name
        self.age = age



user = Person("Alice", 25)
```

We can access the objects attributes using the dot notation – objectName.attribute

```
print(user.name)
print(user.age)
```

We can also access the methods using the dot notation – objectName.method()

```
user.display_info()
```

Lab Exercise 7.1

Create a class called "BankAccount" that models a user's bank account. The class should have the following attributes:

- Account number (a unique identifier)
- Account holder's name
- Account balance

The class should have the following methods:

- **init(self, account_number, account_holder, initial_balance)** This method is the constructor that initializes the account attributes. It takes the account number, account holder's name, and initial balance as parameters.

- **deposit(self, amount)** This method should add the given amount to the account balance.

- **withdraw(self, amount)** This method should subtract the given amount from the account balance. However, it should check if the account has sufficient balance before allowing the withdrawal. If the balance is not sufficient, display an error message.

- **display_info(self)** This method should display the account number, account holder's name, and account balance.

Write a program to implement the class, create some objects and test the methods.

Inheritance

Inheritance is a fundamental concept of object-oriented programming (OOP) that allows you to define a new class based on an existing class. Here in the diagram below, we have a Person class. This is the parent or base class. This class has two child classes: Student and Teacher. These are also known as sub or derived classes.

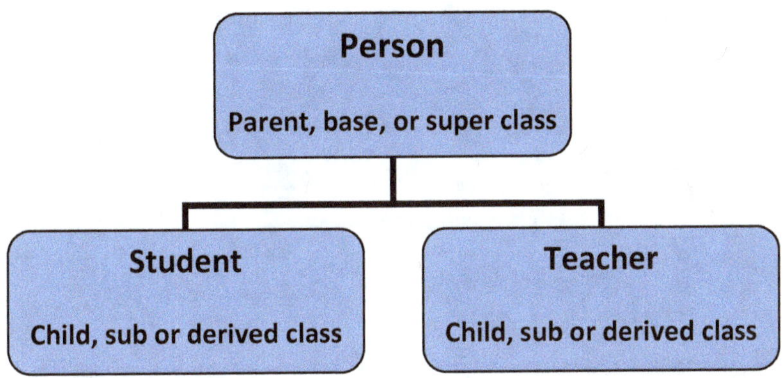

The child class inherits the properties and behaviors (methods) of the existing class or parent class. The child class contains its own unique properties and methods and can sometimes override ones inherited from the parent class.

Defining a Child Class

To create a child class that inherits from a parent, you define the child class using the class keyword, followed by the name of the child class (Student) and the parent class in parentheses (Person). For example, we created the class Person in the previous section, now let's create a child class called Student.

```
class Student(Person):
```

Adding Attributes

Next we need to add the attributes, we can define these inside the __init__() constructor method. We add the parameters we're going to accept in parenthesis.

```
    def __init__(self, name, age, grade):
```

The function super().__init__() calls the constructor of the parent class. This is particularly useful when the parent class has initialization code that you want to execute in the subclass as well. Here we're calling the __init__() constructor method of the parent.

```
super().__init__(name, age)
```

This allows you to initialize the inherited attributes or perform any other necessary setup defined in the parent class.

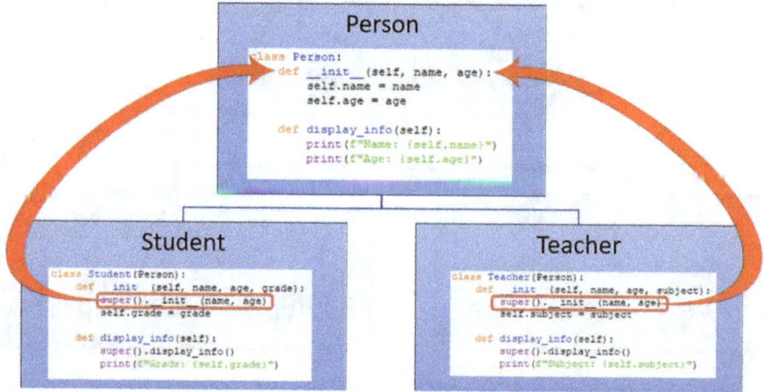

Next we add any other attributes for the child class underneath (eg grade).

```
self.grade = grade
```

Adding Methods

Finally, we add the methods for the child class.

```
def display_info(self):
    super().display_info()
    print(f"Grade: {self.grade}")
```

Creating Objects

We can create some objects using these classes defined above.

```
student1 = Student("Alice", 16, 10)
student2 = Student("Dave", 16, 12)
```

If we want to call a method

```
student1.display_info()
student2.display_info()
```

Lab Exercise 7.2

Create a parent class called "Shape" that represents a geometric shape. The Shape class should have the following attributes:

- Name, Color

The Shape class should also have a method called "display_info()" that prints the shape's name and color.

Next, create two child classes called "Rectangle" and "Circle" that inherit from the Shape class.

The Rectangle class should have additional attributes:

- Width, Height

The Circle class should have an additional attribute:

- Radius

Add a method called "calculate_area()" to the Rectangle and Circle classes to calculate the area. Remember the area of a circle is πr^2 and the area of a rectangle is length x width.

Write a program to implement the class.

Method Overriding

Method overriding allows a child class to provide a different implementation for a method that is already defined in its parent.

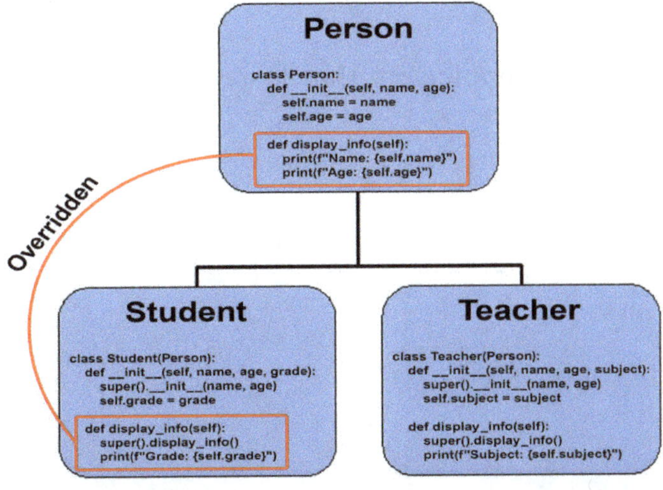

In the diagram on the previous page, the Student class inherits from the parent class Person and adds its own grade attribute. The display_info method in the Student class overrides the method in the Person class.

Lab Exercise 7.3

Define a parent class called "Vehicle" and two child classes called "Car" and "Motorcycle" that inherit from the Vehicle class. The child classes will have their own unique attributes and methods.

The "Vehicle" Class should contains the following attributes:

- brand (string)
- year (integer eg 2014)

Along with the following methods:

- **init()** Initialize the brand and year attributes.
- **display_info()** Print the brand and year of the vehicle.
- **start_engine()** Print a generic message stating that the engine of the vehicle is starting.

Define a child "Car" class that inherits from the "Vehicle" class. The "Car" class should override the start_engine() method to print a specific message for starting a car engine.

Define a child "Motorcycle" class that also inherits from the Vehicle class. The "Motorcycle" class should override the start_engine() method to print a specific message for starting a motorcycle engine.

Write a program to implement the classes.

Polymorphism

Polymorphism is the ability of an object to take on different forms or have multiple types and allows objects of different classes to be treated as objects of a common parent. Polymorphism is achieved through inheritance and method overriding, allowing for the implementation of specialized behavior in child classes. Let's take a look at an example

```
class Device:
    def power_on(self):
        pass

class Smartphone(Device):
    def power_on(self):
        print ("Smartphone is powering on...")

class Laptop(Device):
    def power_on(self):
        print ("Laptop is booting up...")

class SmartTV(Device):
    def power_on(self):
        print ("Smart TV is starting up...")
```

In this example above, we have a parent class Device and three child classes: Smartphone, Laptop, and SmartTV, each representing a different electronic device. Each child class overrides the power_on() method with its specific implementation. We can create some objects using these classes.

```
myphone = Smartphone()
mylaptop = Laptop()
mytv = SmartTV()
```

Each object provides its own implementation of the method, demonstrating polymorphic behavior.

```
myphone.power_on()
mylaptop.power_on()
mytv.power_on()
```

The program determines which power_on() method to use using a mechanism called dynamic dispatch.

When a method is called on an object, the Python interpreter looks for the method implementation in the object's class. If the method is found in the class, it is executed. When myphone.power_on() is called, the Python interpreter recognizes that myphone is an instance of the Smartphone class. It searches for the power_on() method within the Smartphone class and finds it. As a result, the implementation of the power_on() method in the Smartphone class is executed, and the message "Smartphone is powering on..." is printed.

This mechanism allows the program to dynamically dispatch the method calls based on the actual types of the objects at runtime, enabling polymorphic behavior and allowing different objects to have their specific implementations of the same method.

Encapsulation

Encapsulation provides data hiding, abstraction, and encapsulation of related behaviors (methods) into a single unit and is achieved by using access modifiers.

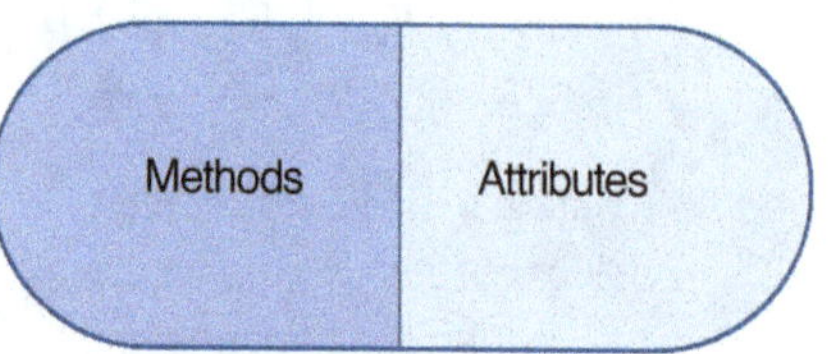

Access Modifiers

Access modifiers are used in define the scope and visibility of class members (the attributes and methods). Python provides three access modifiers:

- Public members are accessible from anywhere, both within and outside the class. By default, all members in Python are public unless specified otherwise.
- Protected members are intended to be accessible only within the class itself and its subclasses. However, Python doesn't enforce strict protection, and the convention is to prefix protected members with a single underscore (_).
- Private members are intended to be accessible only within the class itself. In Python, private members are conventionally prefixed with a double underscore (__).

Let's take a look at an example

```
class BankAccount:
    def __init__(self, account_number, balance):
        self._account_number = account_number
        self.__balance = balance
```

In this example, we have a BankAccount class. It has two attributes: _account_number (protected) and __balance (private).

Getters & Setters

Getter and setter methods, also known as accessors and mutators, are special methods that provide controlled access to the attributes (or properties) of a class. They allow external code to retrieve (get) or modify (set) the values of private or protected attributes, promoting encapsulation and data abstraction.

A getter method is used to retrieve the value of an attribute from a class. It provides read-only access to the attribute by returning its value. They do not take any parameters other than the implicit reference to the instance (self) and return the attribute value. Here we have two getter methods get_account_number() and get_balance() to access the protected attributes in our BankAccount class.

```
    def get_account_number(self):
        return self._account_number

    def get_balance(self):
        return self.__balance
```

A setter method is used to modify the value of an attribute in a class. It provides write access to the attribute by allowing external code to set its value. They take one or more parameters in addition to the implicit reference to the instance (self) and update the attribute value. Here we have two setter methods deposit() and withdraw() to modify the private __balance attribute.

```
    def deposit(self, amount):
        if amount > 0:
            self.__balance += amount

    def withdraw(self, amount):
        if amount > 0 and amount <= self.__balance:
            self.__balance -= amount
```

Lab Exercises 7.4

1. What is object-oriented programming (OOP)? How does it differ from procedural programming?
2. What is the purpose of creating a parent class (such as Shape) in object-oriented programming?
3. Explain the concept of inheritance in object-oriented programming. How does it allow child classes to inherit properties and behaviors from the parent class?
4. Create a class called Shape with a method area() that calculates and returns the area of the shape.
5. Implement this class as the parent class and create child classes such as Circle, Square, and Triangle that inherit from the Shape class. Each child class should override the area() method to provide its specific implementation.
6. Create objects of each child class and calculate their respective areas.
7. What is encapsulation?
8. What is polymorphism?
9. What is method overriding?

Summary

- Object-oriented programming (OOP) in Python involves modeling real-world scenarios using objects and their interactions.
- Python provides syntax for defining classes, creating objects, and implementing OOP concepts such as inheritance, encapsulation, polymorphism, and abstraction.
- A class is a blueprint for creating objects, defining their attributes (data) and methods (behaviors).
- An object is an instance of a class that represents a specific entity with its own unique data and behaviors.

- Attributes are variables that hold data associated with an object, and methods are functions defined within a class that perform actions on the object's data.
- Encapsulation bundles data and methods within a class, allowing for data hiding and providing a clear interface for interacting with objects.
- Inheritance allows a class to inherit attributes and methods from another class, creating a hierarchy of classes.
- Polymorphism enables objects of different classes to be treated as objects of a common parent, allowing for specialized behavior in child classes.
- Abstraction simplifies complex systems by breaking them down into manageable components, focusing on essential characteristics while hiding unnecessary details.
- Defining a class involves using the class keyword followed by the class name, along with attributes and methods.
- Objects can be created by calling the class name followed by parentheses, and their attributes and methods can be accessed using dot notation.
- Method overriding allows a child class to provide a different implementation for a method already defined in its parent class.
- Polymorphism is achieved through inheritance and method overriding, allowing objects of different classes to have their specific implementations of the same method.
- Encapsulation provides data hiding, abstraction, and encapsulation of behaviors, and is achieved using access modifiers such as public, protected, and private.
- Getter and setter methods provide controlled access to attributes, allowing read-only or write access to private or protected attributes.
- Getter methods retrieve attribute values, while setter methods modify attribute values.

8

Modules & Libraries

Modules and libraries are used to organize and distribute reusable pieces of code. A module is a single file containing Python definitions, statements, and functions, while a library is a collection of modules that can be used to solve specific problems or perform certain tasks.

Python provides a rich ecosystem of built-in modules and libraries, covering a wide range of functionalities such as mathematics, file handling, networking, web development, data analysis, and graphics. These are known as standard libraries.

Additionally, third-party libraries can be installed using package managers such as pip to extend the capabilities of Python even further.

For this chapter, you'll need to download the source code files from:

`elluminetpress.com/pymod`

You'll also find various video demos and tutorials.

Commonly Used Libraries

There are numerous commonly used modules in Python's standard library and popular third-party libraries.

- **NumPy** is a library for numerical computing in Python, providing powerful data structures and operations for multidimensional arrays and matrices.
- **Pandas** is a library for data manipulation and analysis, providing high-performance data structures and data analysis tools.
- **Turtle** is a graphics is a popular graphics library in Python that allows you to create drawings, animations, and games using a virtual "turtle" that can move around the screen.
- **Pygame** is a library for building games and multimedia applications, providing functionality for graphics rendering, sound playback, and user input handling.
- **Tkinter** is the standard Python interface to the Tk GUI toolkit. It provides a set of tools for building graphical user interfaces, including various widgets (buttons, labels, entry fields, etc.) that you can use to create windows, dialogs, and other GUI elements.
- **PyQt** is a set of Python bindings for the Qt application framework. It allows you to create cross-platform GUI applications with rich functionality and a modern look and feel. PyQt provides a wide range of widgets and tools for building desktop applications.
- **PyTorch** is another deep learning library that offers a flexible and dynamic approach to building neural networks, with a focus on research and experimentation.
- **Django** is a powerful web framework for building web applications, providing tools and libraries for handling routing, database management, user authentication, and more.
- **Flask** is a lightweight web framework that focuses on simplicity and extensibility, making it suitable for building small to medium-sized web applications and APIs.

- **Pickle** allows serialization and deserialization of Python objects.
- **Gzip** allows reading and writing of files in GZIP compressed format.
- **Zipfile** provides functionality for creating, reading, and extracting files from ZIP archives.
- **Urllib** enables making HTTP requests and working with URLs.
- **Socket** allows low-level network communication, such as creating sockets and sending/receiving data over a network.
- **Email** provides functionality for creating, sending, and parsing email messages.
- **Json** facilitates working with JSON data, including encoding and decoding JSON objects.
- **Math** provides mathematical functions and constants for numerical calculations.
- **Datetime** enables working with dates, times, and time intervals.
- **Os** offers functions for interacting with the operating system, such as file operations and directory manipulation.
- **Random** allows generating random numbers and making random selections.

Importing Libraries

To use any of these libraries in your programs, you'll need to import them. To do this use the import keyword followed by the library name. For example

```
import random
```

To call a function from an imported module or library use

```
moduleName.function()
```

For example if we wanted to write a program that generates a random number, we first import the random library.

```
import random
random_number = random.randint(1, 10)
print("Random Number:", random_number)
```

In this example, we use the random.randint() function to generate a random integer between 1 and 10 (inclusive). Finally, we print the generated random number.

Here's another example that imports the datetime module.

```
import datetime
current_datetime = datetime.datetime.now()
print("Current Date and Time:", current_datetime)
```

In this example, we import the datetime module using the import statement. We then use the datetime.datetime.now() function to get the current date and time. Finally, we print the current date and time.

Creating your Own Libraries

By creating a library, you can package and encapsulate your code into reusable modules. This allows you to avoid duplicating code across multiple projects and breaks down complex tasks into smaller, more manageable components making it easier to understand, maintain, and update. You can declare and store your functions in a separate file and import them into your main program.

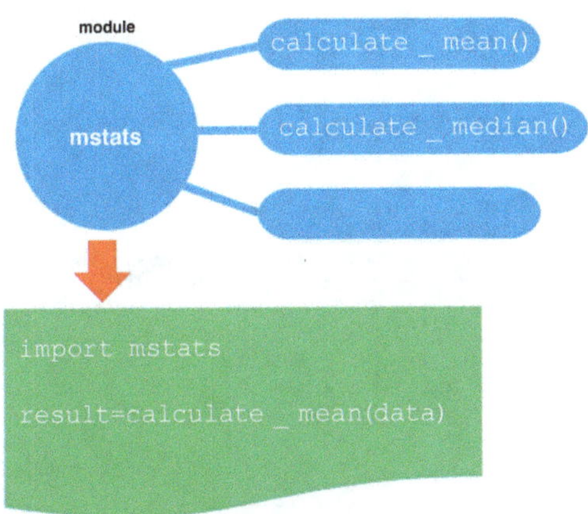

For example, let's say we've written some functions to calculate the mean and median of some numbers. To use these functions in other programs, we can save them in a separate python file (such as mstats.py).

```
def calculate_mean(data):
    return sum(data) / len(data)

def calculate_median(data):
    sorted_data = sorted(data)
    n = len(sorted_data)
    if n % 2 == 0:
        mid1 = sorted_data[n // 2 - 1]
        mid2 = sorted_data[n // 2]
        median = (mid1 + mid2) / 2
    else:
        median = sorted_data[n // 2]
    return median
```

In our program we import the mstats library we created above.

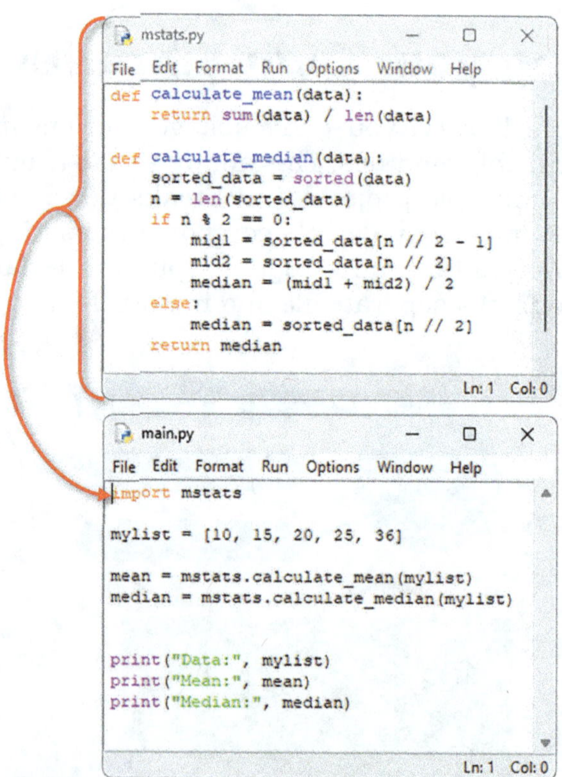

This is just the name of the file without the .py extension.

```
import mstats
```

Here we have a list that contains a series of integers for which we want to calculate the mean and median.

```
mylist = [10, 15, 20, 25, 36]
```

To call the function from the mstats library, we need to state the library name, followed by the function we want.

```
libraryName.functionName()
```

In this example mstats is the library name and the function we want from this library is calculate_mean(), so we get mstats. calculate_mean(mylist). This calls the calculate_mean() function from the mstats module and passes mylist as an argument. This function calculates the mean of the numbers in the list results the result.

```
mean = mstats.calculate_mean(mylist)
```

When we execute the program

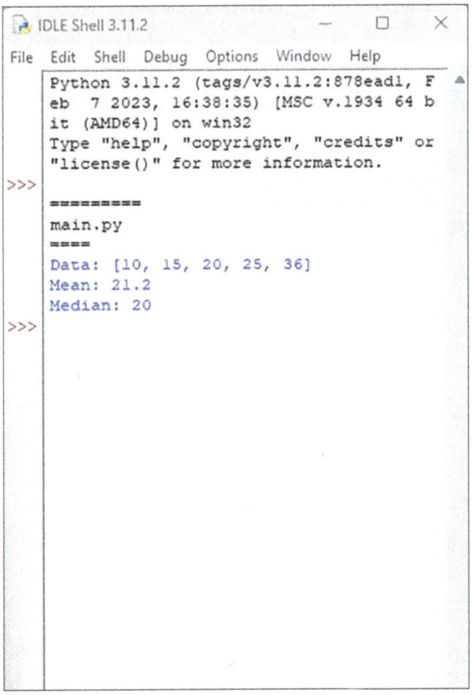

```
IDLE Shell 3.11.2
File  Edit  Shell  Debug  Options  Window  Help
Python 3.11.2 (tags/v3.11.2:878ead1, F
eb  7 2023, 16:38:35) [MSC v.1934 64 b
it (AMD64)] on win32
Type "help", "copyright", "credits" or
"license()" for more information.
>>>
=========
main.py
====
Data: [10, 15, 20, 25, 36]
Mean: 21.2
Median: 20
>>>
```

Lab Exercises 8.1

1. What is the purpose of modules and libraries in Python?
2. How is a module different from a library?
3. What are standard libraries in Python?
4. How can you extend the capabilities of Python by using third-party libraries?
5. Name some commonly used libraries in Python's standard library.
6. How do you import a library into a program?
7. Create a new Python file called "num_operations.py". Write a function called "calculate_average(numbers)" that takes a list of numbers as input and returns the average (mean).
8. Write another function called "find_maximum(numbers)" that takes a list of numbers as input and returns the maximum.
9. Test your functions by calling them with different sets of numbers in a separate Python file.

Summary

- Modules and libraries are used to organize and distribute reusable pieces of code.
- A module is a single file containing Python definitions, statements, and functions, while a library is a collection of modules.
- Python provides built-in modules and libraries known as standard libraries, covering various functionalities.
- Commonly used libraries include NumPy, Pandas, Turtle, Pygame, Tkinter, PyQt, PyTorch, Django, Flask, Pickle, Gzip, Zipfile, Urllib, Socket, Email, Json, Math, Datetime, Os, and Random.
- Third-party libraries can be installed using package managers like pip to extend Python's capabilities.
- Libraries need to be imported into programs using the import keyword, followed by the library name.
- Functions from imported libraries can be called using the syntax libraryName.function().
- Creating your own libraries allows you to package and encapsulate your code into reusable modules.
- You can declare and store functions in a separate file and import them into your main program.
- Custom libraries can be imported and used in other programs using the import statement followed by the library name - usually the filename without the .py extension.
- Calling functions from a custom library requires using the library name followed by the function name, like libraryName.functionName().
- Libraries are continuously updated to introduce new features and fix bugs. It's important to keep your libraries up to date by checking for updates and installing newer versions when available. However, be cautious with major updates as they may introduce changes that can break your code.

9

Graphics and GUIs

Creating graphics and GUIs (Graphical User Interfaces) in Python involves the use of libraries specifically designed for this purpose. Tkinter is a built-in Python library for creating GUI applications. It provides a set of tools and widgets to build windows, buttons, text boxes, menus, and so on. Tkinter is easy to learn and widely used for creating simple GUIs.

PyQt is a popular cross-platform library for creating GUI applications. It provides a rich set of tools and widgets to build professional-looking user interfaces. PyQt offers extensive documentation and allows you to create both simple and complex GUI applications.

For this chapter, you'll need to download the source code files from:

`elluminetpress.com/pygui`

You'll also find various video demos and tutorials.

Using Tkinter

Tkinter is a built-in Python library for creating GUI applications. It provides a set of tools and widgets to build windows, buttons, text boxes, and menus.

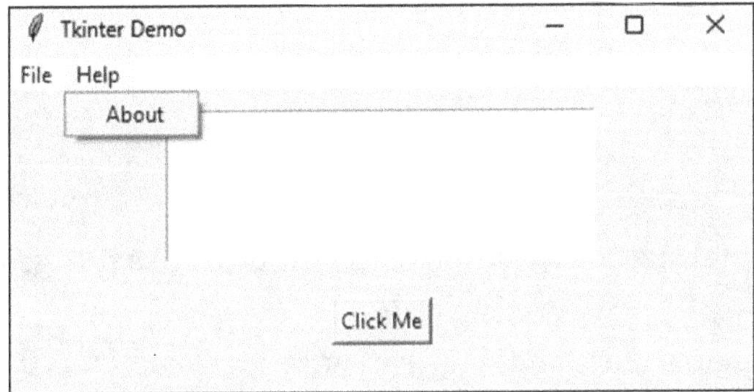

To start using this module, you'll first need to install it. Open up the command prompt, then type the following command to install Tkinter.

```
pip install tk
```

You'll see a confirmation in the command prompt window once complete.

```
Administrator: Command Prompt
Microsoft Windows [Version 10.0.22621.1778]
(c) Microsoft Corporation. All rights reserved.

C:\Windows\System32>pip install tk
Collecting tk
  Downloading tk-0.1.0-py3-none-any.whl (3.9 kB)
Installing collected packages: tk
Successfully installed tk-0.1.0

[notice] A new release of pip available: 22.3.1 -> 23.1.2
[notice] To update, run: python.exe -m pip install --upgrade pip

C:\Windows\System32>_
```

Creating a Window

The first thing you need to do is import the tkinter module into your program. To do this, use

```
from tkinter import *
```

To create a window use the Tk() method

```
window = Tk()
Add a title
window.title("Window Title")
```

Set the initial size and position of the window. Use the .geometry() method.

```
window.geometry("800x600+50+20")
```

The first two numbers in this case '800x600', sets the window size. Set this to the desired window size in pixels. This could be 1280x720, 1920x1080, and so on.

The second two numbers in this case '50+20', sets the initial position of the window on the screen using x and y co-ordinates. We've also added a window title. You can do this using the .title() method. This helps to identify your app.

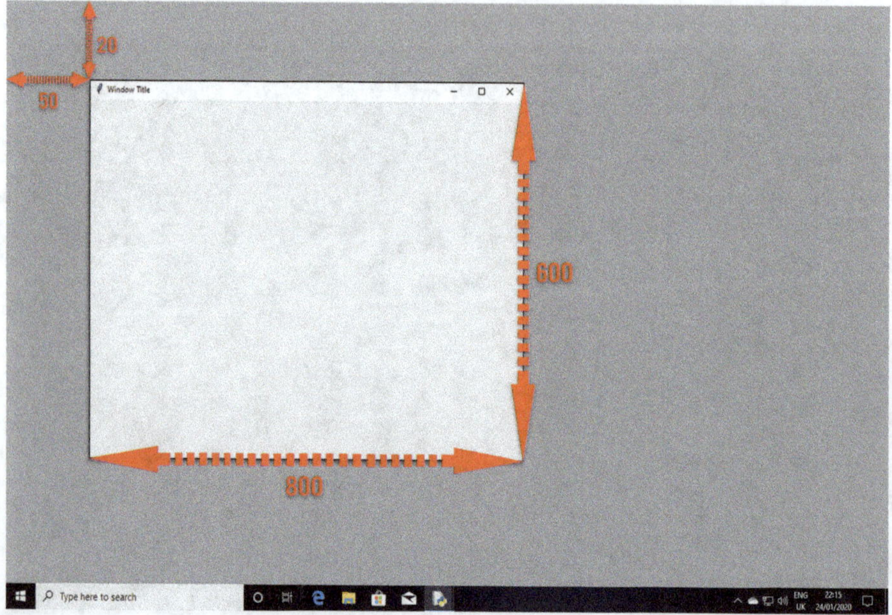

Finally to make the window appear, we need to enter the Tkinter event loop. You can do this with the .mainloop() method.

```
window.mainloop()
```

This is an infinite loop used to run the application and is called an event loop. The .mainloop() method waits for an event such as a key press, or mouse click events from the window system and dispatches them to the application widgets (frames, buttons, menus, etc).

When you run the program, you'll see a blank window appear on the screen.

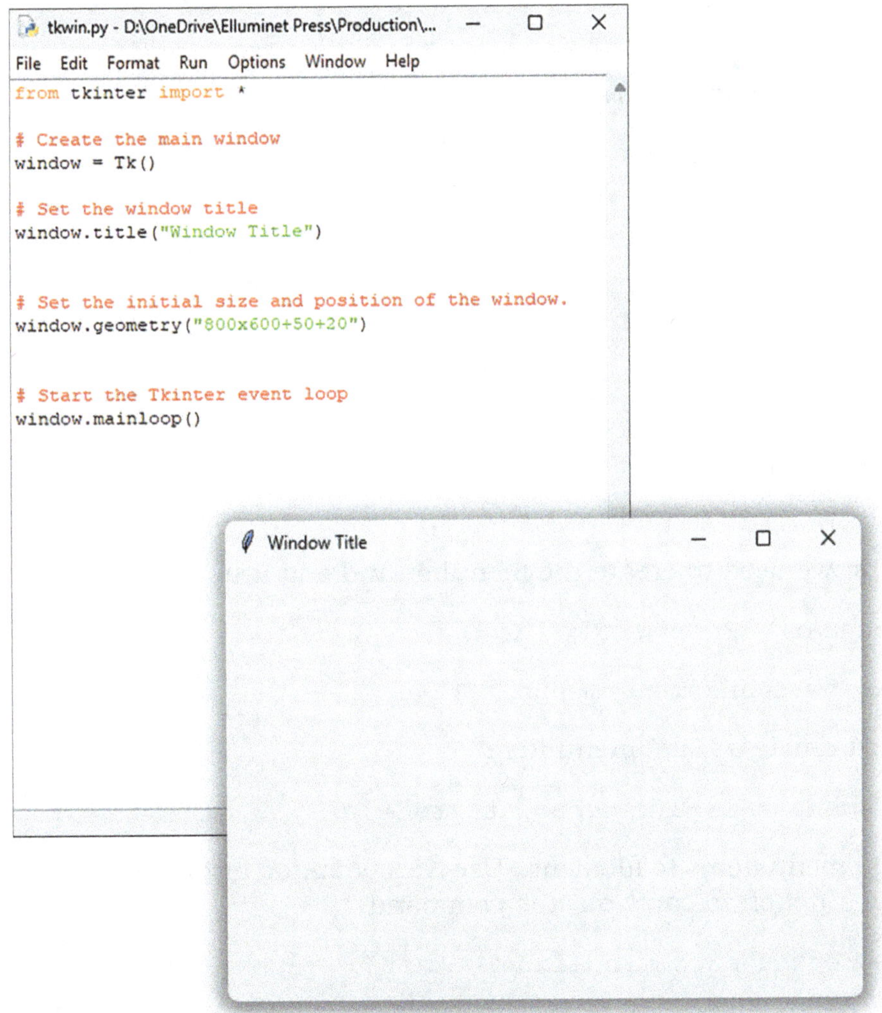

Adding Widgets

Widgets are standard items for building a graphic user interface using Tkinter.

Menus

Let's add a menu. You can create a menu bar using the Menu() function. Assign it to an object (eg menubar) and attach it to your main window.

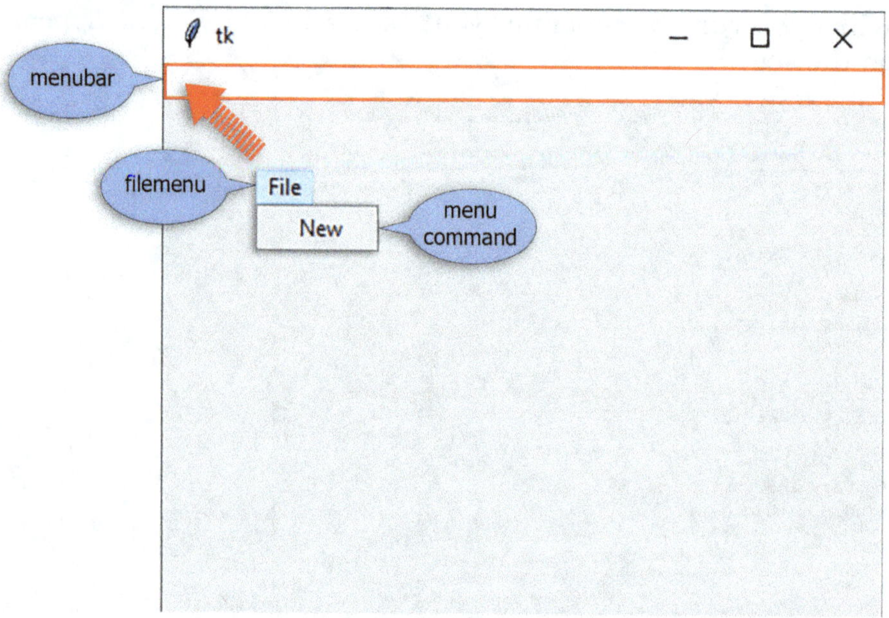

First we need to create the menubar and add it to the window

```
menubar = Menu(window)
```

```
window.config(menu=menubar)
```

Next create a "File" menu item.

```
filemenu = Menu(menubar, tearoff=0)
```

Add menu items to filemenu. Use the command argument to call the function to carry out the command.

```
filemenu.add_command(label="Exit",
                                 command=newb)
```

Add filemenu to the menu bar.

```
menubar.add_cascade(label="File", menu=filemenu)
```

Finally, for each menu item, you need to define a function to deal with what the menu item does.

```
filemenu.add_command(label="Exit", command=endit)
```

Make sure the function is defined at the top of the program

```
def endit():
    print ('Program Exiting...')
```

When you run the program, you'll see the menu bar appear along the top of the window.

Buttons

You can add command buttons to your canvas. To do this use the Button() function.

```
myButton = Button(window, text="label", command)
```

Use window to specify the name of the window the button is to go on.

Use command to specify the function you want to call to handle what the button does. You can call existing functions or define your own functions to do this.

Use the .place method to add the button to your window at specific x & y coordinates.

```
myButton.place(x=100, y=100)
```

Text Field

Use the Entry() function to create your text field.

```
userInput = Entry( window )
```

Use the .pack() method to add the field to your window.

```
userInput.pack()
```

To get the data from the text field use the .get() method

```
userInput.get()
```

We've also added code in the dialog() function to get the data from the text field and display it in a message box.

The dialog() function is called when the 'click me' button is pressed.

Run the program and see what it does.

Listbox

Use the Listbox() function to create your list box.

```
list = Listbox(window)
```

Use the .insert() method to add items to the listbox.

```
list.insert(1, 'Item One')
```

Use the .pack() method to add the listbox to your window.

Use the padx and pady parameters to add some padding to space out your listbox in the window.

```
list.pack(padx=20, pady=20)
```

Use the .curselection() method to get the index of the item selected by the user. Remember, the first item's index is 0.

```
selectedItem = list.curselection()
```

Use the .get() method to return the item

```
list.get (selectedItem)
```

Checkbox

Use the Checkbutton()function to create each of your checkboxes.

```
box1 = Checkbutton(window, text="Red",
       variable=box1Checked, onvalue=1)
```

You'll need to create a variable for each checkbox to assign its 'onvalue' if the user clicks the checkbox.

```
box1Checked = IntVar()
```

The variables you created above will either be 1 or 0. Onvalue is set to 1, so the variable will be set to 1 when the user clicks the checkbox. Use the .get() method to get the value.

```
   if box1Checked.get() == 1:
      messagebox.showinfo( 'Msg' , "Red" )
```

Use the .pack() method to add each of your checkboxes to your window.

```
box1.pack()
```

Labels

You can create labels to label text fields and other items on your interface. To do this, use Label()

```
textLabel = Label(window, text="Enter Name:")
```

Use pack() to add the label to your window.

```
textLabel.pack()
```

Label Frame

The LabelFrame is used to group related widgets.

You can group checkboxes, radiobuttons or text fields. First you need to create your label frame group. You can do this with LabelFrame() as follows

```
group1 = LabelFrame(window, text="label",
        padx=5, pady=5)
```

Use the first parameter window to attach the group to your main window. Next you need to add your widgets to your group. You can do this in the usual way, except you need to specify in the widget functions, which widget to attach to.

So to add our text label, specify the widget to attach to using the first parameter (our labelframe defined above is called group1, so use group1 underlined below).

```
textLabel = Label(group1, text="Name: ")
```

Add your widgets to your window in the usual way.

```
textLabel.pack(side=LEFT)
```

Images and the Canvas

The canvas is used to draw, create graphics, and layouts. This is where you place your graphics, text, buttons and other widgets to create your interface.

To create a canvas use:

```
myCanvas = Tkinter.Canvas (parent-window,
    bg="sky blue", height=300, width=300)
```

Use parent-window to attach the canvas to your window. Use height and width to size your canvas. Select the name of the color from the chart to use in the bg parameter.

You can add images to your canvas. Have a look at images.py.

To load the image use the PhotoImage() function.

```
img = PhotoImage(file="rocket.png")
```

To size the image use .subsample. X and Y will scaled down the image by a factor of 6 in both the horizontal and vertical directions

```
PhotoImage.subsample(img, x=6, y=6)
```

To paste the image on your canvas use the .create_image() method. Supply the X and Y co-ordinates. This is where you want to place the top-left corner of the image item on the canvas.

In this case, the image item will be positioned at (20, 60) pixels from the top-left corner of the canvas. Anchor specifies the anchor point for the image item. In this case, NW stands for "northwest" and means that the image item is positioned relative to the top-left corner of the image. Img represents the image object or image file that you want to display.

```
myCanvas.create_image(20,60, anchor=NW, image=img)
```

Here below we can see the image has been added to the canvas.

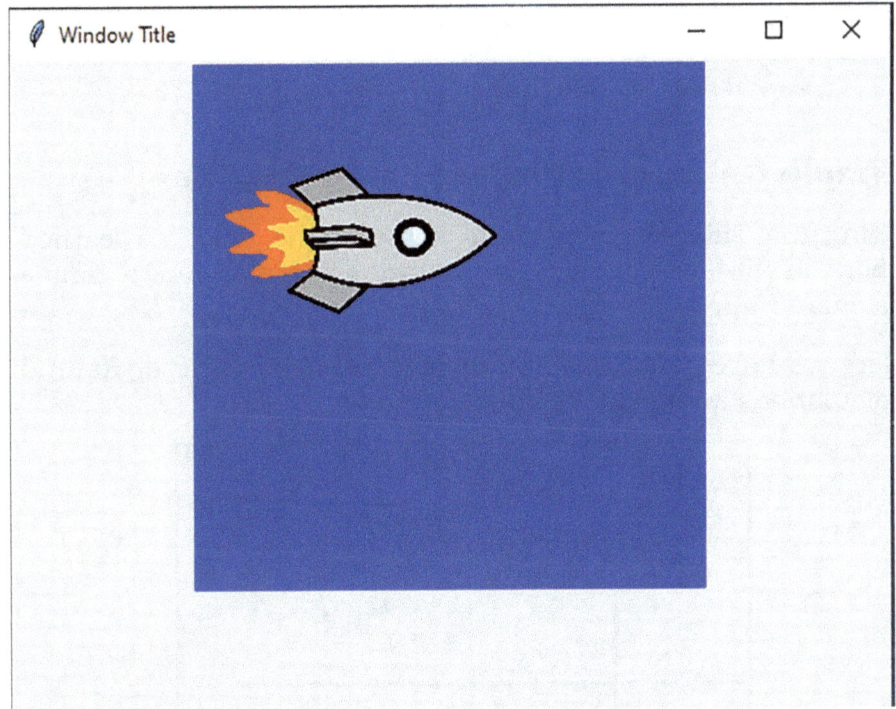

Message Boxes

You can add message boxes to your programs. To do this you will need to import the messagebox functions from the tkinter module.

You can to this using the import command.

```
from tkinter import messagebox
```

You can create different types of message boxes. An info box, a warning box, an error box, and a box that asks for a yes/no response.

```
messagebox.showinfo('Message Title', 'Message')
```

If you're asking the user for a yes/no response, you'll need to process this.

```
response = messagebox.askquestion
          ('Message Box' , 'Question...')

if response == 'yes' :
     executed if user clicks 'yes'
else :
     executed if user clicks 'no'
```

Simple Calculator Project using Tkinter

Using the Tkinter module and some of the tools we learned about in the previous section, we are going to create a simple calculator app.

Here we have a text field at the top to display the digits and calculations and a grid of buttons below.

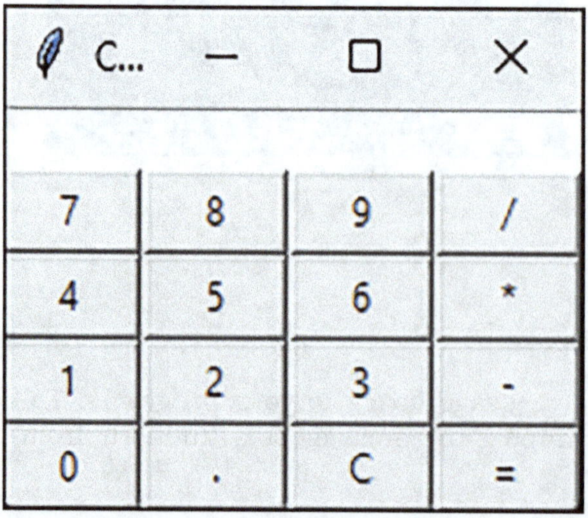

First, we need to design the interface. Here, we want to create a window that spans 4 columns and 5 rows.

We want a text entry widget at the top to display the expression we are trying to calculate. This is in row 0.

The digits and the operators will be represented by buttons and arranged in a 4x4 grid. This will start on row 1 and end on row 4. You can see this in the figure below.

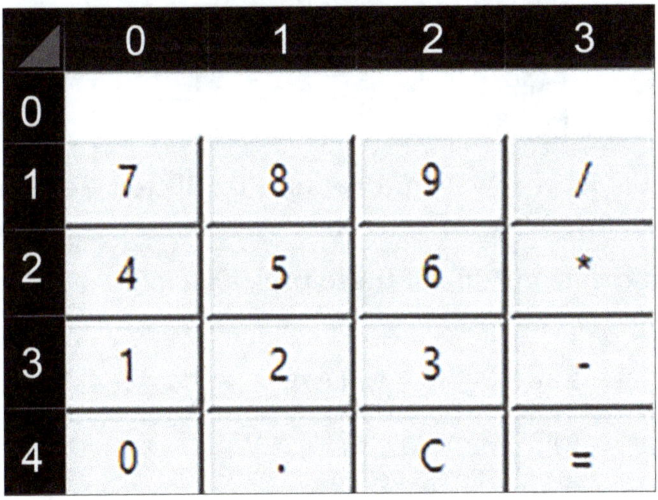

	0	1	2	3
0				
1	7	8	9	/
2	4	5	6	*
3	1	2	3	-
4	0	.	C	=

Let's start building the app

Import the tkinter module and alias it as tk for convenience.

```
import tkinter as tk
```

Create a Tkinter window using the Tk() constructor and set the title of the window to "Calculator".

```
window = tk.Tk()
window.title("Calculator")
```

Create an text entry widget to display the input and output of the calculator. It is placed at row 0, column 0, and spans 4 columns.

```
entry = tk.Entry(window, width=30)
entry.grid(row=0, column=0, columnspan=4)
```

Create a list of tuples representing the buttons on the calculator.

Each tuple consists of the button label, row position, and column position.

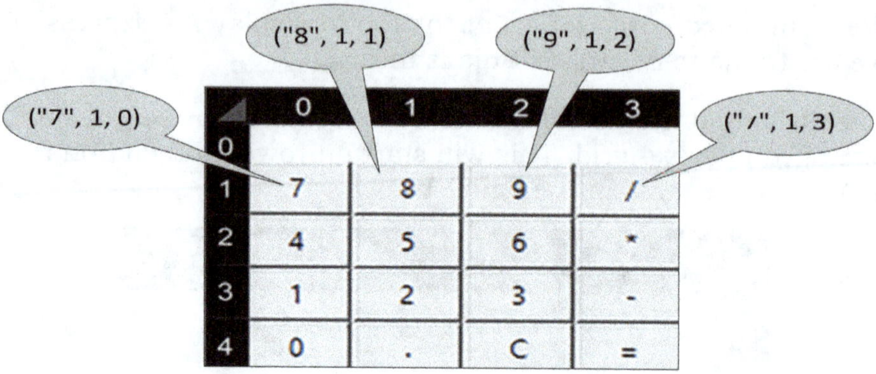

So button 7 is in row 1 and column 0. Button 8 is on row 1, column 1, and so on.

So we can create our list of these tuples as follows

```
buttons = [
    ("7", 1, 0), ("8", 1, 1), ("9", 1, 2), ("/", 1, 3),
    ("4", 2, 0), ("5", 2, 1), ("6", 2, 2), ("*", 2, 3),
    ("1", 3, 0), ("2", 3, 1), ("3", 3, 2), ("-", 3, 3),
    ("0", 4, 0), (".", 4, 1), ("=", 4, 2), ("+", 4, 3)
]
```

Iterate over the buttons list to create a button for each tuple in the list. We can do this using a for loop.

```
for btn_text, row, col in buttons:
    button = tk.Button(window, text=btn_text,
        width=5, command=lambda text=btn_text:
        entry.insert(tk.END, text))
```

window specifies the parent window or frame where the button will be placed.

text=btn_text sets the text displayed on the button. The value of btn_text is assigned to the text parameter.

width=5 specifies the width of the button, in characters.

command=lambda text=btn_text: entry.insert(tk.END, text) sets the command or function to be executed when the button is clicked.

In this case, a lambda function is used. The lambda function takes button's text (btn_text), and it inserts the value at the end of the text entry widget (entry) using the insert method.

Next, create a button for clearing the text entry widget by deleting its contents ("C").

```
clear_button = tk.Button(window, text="C", width=5,
            command=lambda: entry.delete(0, tk.END))
```

Create an "=" button for performing the calculation by calling the calculate() function.

```
equal_button = tk.Button(window, text="=", width=5,
                command=calculate)
```

Use the grid() method to position the "C" button at row 4, column 2, and the "=" button at row 4, column 3.

```
clear_button.grid(row=4, column=2)
equal_button.grid(row=4, column=3)
```

Now to make the calculator work we need to define a calculate() function that retrieves the expression from the text entry widget, evaluates it using the eval() function, then displays the result back in the text entry widget. If an exception occurs during evaluation, it displays an error message.

def calculate():

```
    try:
        expression = entry.get()
        result = eval(expression)
        entry.delete(0, tk.END)
        entry.insert(tk.END, str(result))
    except Exception as e:
        entry.delete(0, tk.END)
        entry.insert(tk.END, "Error")
```

Start the main event loop using the mainloop() method of the Tkinter window, which allows the application to handle user interactions and events.

```
window.mainloop()
```

From the Chapter 09 folder, have a look at calc.py

Using PyQt

To create apps using PyQT, you'll first need to install it. To do this, open up the command prompt, then type the following command to install PyQT.

```
pip install PyQt5
```

Once installed, you'll see a confirmation in the command prompt window.

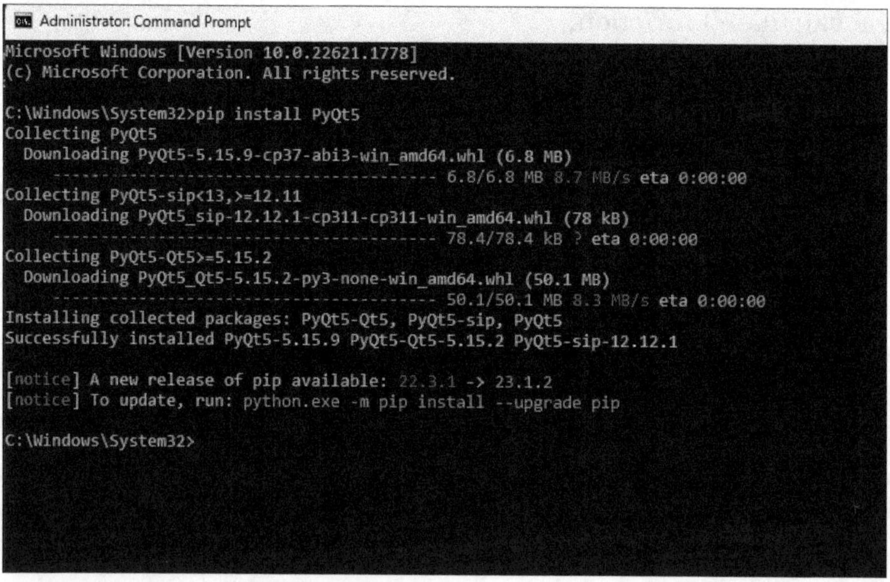

```
Administrator: Command Prompt
Microsoft Windows [Version 10.0.22621.1778]
(c) Microsoft Corporation. All rights reserved.

C:\Windows\System32>pip install PyQt5
Collecting PyQt5
  Downloading PyQt5-5.15.9-cp37-abi3-win_amd64.whl (6.8 MB)
     ---------------------------------------- 6.8/6.8 MB 8.7 MB/s eta 0:00:00
Collecting PyQt5-sip<13,>=12.11
  Downloading PyQt5_sip-12.12.1-cp311-cp311-win_amd64.whl (78 kB)
     ---------------------------------------- 78.4/78.4 kB ? eta 0:00:00
Collecting PyQt5-Qt5>=5.15.2
  Downloading PyQt5_Qt5-5.15.2-py3-none-win_amd64.whl (50.1 MB)
     ---------------------------------------- 50.1/50.1 MB 8.3 MB/s eta 0:00:00
Installing collected packages: PyQt5-Qt5, PyQt5-sip, PyQt5
Successfully installed PyQt5-5.15.9 PyQt5-Qt5-5.15.2 PyQt5-sip-12.12.1

[notice] A new release of pip available: 22.3.1 -> 23.1.2
[notice] To update, run: python.exe -m pip install --upgrade pip

C:\Windows\System32>
```

Creating a Window

The first thing you need to do is import the PyQt modules into your program. To do this, use

```
import sys
from PyQt5.QtWidgets import QApplication, QMainWindow
```

To create a window use the QMainWindow method

```
app = QApplication(sys.argv)
window = QMainWindow()
window.setWindowTitle("PyQt Demo")
```

Set the window size and position.

The first two arguments are the x and y coordinates of the top left corner of the window on the screen, while the second two arguments mark the size of the window.

```
window.setGeometry(100, 100, 400, 300)
```

Make the window visible.

```
window.show()
```

When we execute the program, we'll end up with this:

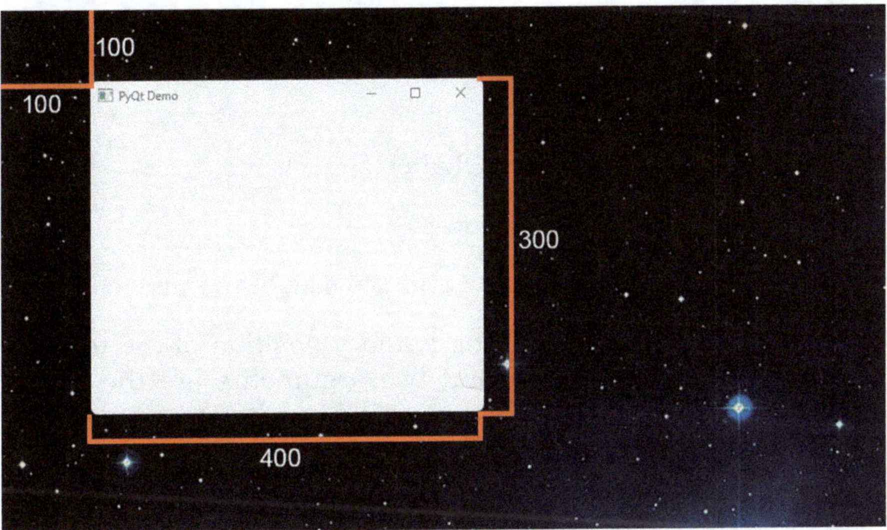

Have a look at qtdemo.py in the Ch09 folder.

Menus

You can add menus to the window. First create the menu bar.

```
menu_bar = window.menuBar()
```

Create the actual menu to appear on the bar. You can create one of these for each menu that appears along the menu bar

```
file_menu = menu_bar.addMenu("File")
```

Create menu items for each menu created above

```
exit_action = QAction("Exit", window)
exit_action.triggered.connect(window.close)
```

Add the menu item to the menu

```
file_menu.addAction(exit_action)
```

Have a look at pyqtmenu.py in the Ch09 folder

Images

To add images first create a QLabel widget to display the image

```
image_label = QLabel(window)
```

Next, load the image using QPixmap

```
pixmap = QPixmap('rocket.png')
```

Add the image pixmap to the QLabel

```
image_label.setPixmap(pixmap)
```

Now set position in the window and the size of the image.

The first two arguments are the x and y position of the top left corner of the image, the second two arguments are the width and height of the image itself.

```
image_label.setGeometry(50, 50, pixmap.width(),
    pixmap.height())
```

Have a loot at qtimage.py in the Ch09 folder

Buttons

To add a button to the code, you can use the QPushButton widget.

First create the button. Put the button text in the first argument, and the window you want to add the button to in the second argument.

```
button = QPushButton("Click Me", window)
```

Next, set button position and size

```
button.setGeometry(150, 150, 100, 50)
```

Once you have created the button, add a click event and pass the function name as an argument.

```
button.clicked.connect(button_clicked)
```

Have a look at qtbutton in the Ch09 folder.

Message Boxes

To add message boxes for your messages, you can use the QMessageBox widget. The first argument is the window you want to add the message box to, the second argument is the message box title and the third argument is the actual message that will be displayed in the message box.

```
QMessageBox.information(window, "Alert", "Button clicked!")
```

You can add different types of message boxes.

Information Box (QMessageBox.information) displays an informational message to the user.

```
QMessageBox.information(window, "Info",
                        "Button clicked!")
```

Warning Box (QMessageBox.warning) shows a warning message to alert the user about a potential issue or problem.

```
QMessageBox.warning(window, "Alert",
                        "Button clicked!")
```

Error Box (QMessageBox.critical) displays an error message to indicate an error or critical condition.

```
QMessageBox.critical(window, "Warning",
                        "Button clicked!")
```

Question Box (QMessageBox.question) prompts the user with a yes/no question and returns the user's response.

To use this box, you'll need to insert code to deal with the user's response, either yes or no.

So for example

```
reply = QMessageBox.question(window, "Confirmation",
        "Are you sure you want to proceed?",
        QMessageBox.Yes | QMessageBox.No)

if reply == QMessageBox.Yes:
    QMessageBox.information(window, "Response", "Yes!")

else:
    QMessageBox.information(window, "Response", "No!")
```

Have a look at qtmessagebox.py in the Ch09 folder.

Text Field

To add a text field (QLineEdit) to the code, you can use the QLineEdit widget.

First, create a QLineEdit widget

```
text_field = QLineEdit(window)
```

Set text field position and size.

```
text_field.setGeometry(50, 50, 300, 30)
```

Have a look at qttextfield.py in the Ch09 folder

Listbox

To add a list box (QListWidget) to the code, you can use the QListWidget widget

First create a QListWidget

```
list_box = QListWidget(window)
Set list box position and size
list_box.setGeometry(50, 50, 300, 200)
```

Add items to the list box

```
list_box.addItem("Item 1")
list_box.addItem("Item 2")
list_box.addItem("Item 3")
```

Next you need to add the code that will process the selections.

Connect the function to the itemClicked signal.

```
list_box.itemClicked.connect(function)
```

Have a look at qtlistbox.py in the Ch09 Folder

Checkbox

To add a checkbox (QCheckBox) to the existing code, you can use the QCheckBox widget.

```
checkbox = QCheckBox("Enable", window)
```

Set checkbox position and size

```
checkbox.setGeometry(50, 50, 100, 30)
```

Connect checkbox state change to a function

```
checkbox.stateChanged.connect(function)
```

Have a look at qtcheckbox.py in the Ch09 folder.

Labels

To add a label (QLabel) to the existing code, you can use the QLabel widget

First create the label using QLabel

```
label = QLabel("This is a label", window)
```

Set label position and size

```
label.setGeometry(50, 50, 200, 30)
```

Have a look at qtlabels.py in the Ch09 folder.

Simple Unit Converter Project using PyQt

Let's design a simple interface for a unit converter app. We want the user to be able to select the conversions from a combo box. We also want the user to be able to type in the unit for conversion and a command button to execute the command. Finally we need a label to display the actual conversions.

To design this interface, we'll divide the window up into 4 rows and 3 columns. Each of the elements will be positioned in the grid as shown below.

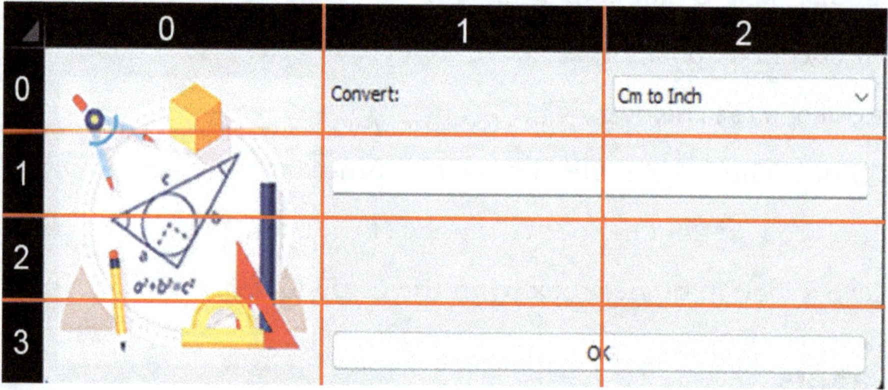

First let's create a window.

```
app = QApplication(sys.argv)

window = QMainWindow()
window.setWindowTitle("Unit Converter")
window.setGeometry(500, 20, 525, 180)

widget = QWidget(window)
window.setCentralWidget(widget)

layout = QGridLayout()
widget.setLayout(layout)
```

Next, we want to create the interface we designed in figure 11. First let's add the image on the left hand side.

```
imgLabel = QLabel()
pixmap = QPixmap("logo.png")
imgLabel.setPixmap(pixmap)
```

This image starts at column 0 and row 0, spans 4 rows and 1 column.

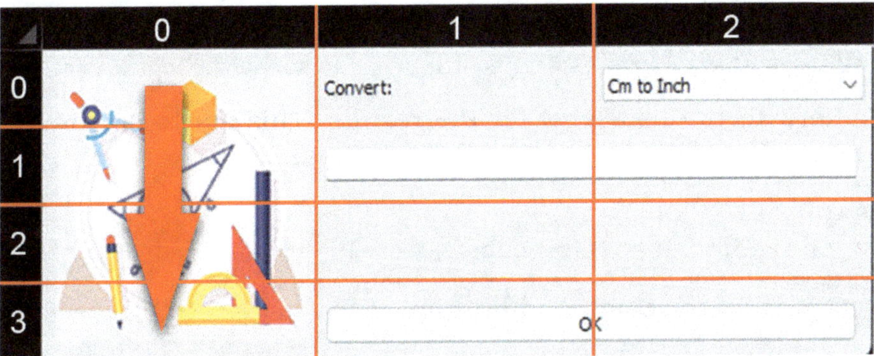

To do this we add the line. The first argument is the object being added to the layout. Followed by the row and column index where the widget will go. The last two arguments indicate how many rows and columns the widget should span. In this case 4 rows and 1 column.

```
layout.addWidget(imgLabel, 0, 0, 4, 1)
```

Add a convert label

```
textLabel = QLabel("Convert:")
```

This label is on row 0 and column 1.

```
layout.addWidget(textLabel, 0, 1)
```

Add the combo box

```
conversions = QComboBox()

conversions.addItems([
    "Cm to Inch",
    "Inch to Cm",
    "Km to Miles",
    "Miles to Km"

])
```

The combo box is on row 0 column 2

```
layout.addWidget(conversions, 0, 2)
```

Next is the user input text box. This starts on row 1, column 1 and spans 1 row and 2 columns.

```
userInput = QLineEdit()
layout.addWidget(userInput, 1, 1, 1, 2)
```

Same with the text label for the results. This starts on row 2, column 1 and spans 1 row and 2 columns.

```
textLabel = QLabel()
layout.addWidget(textLabel, 2, 1, 1, 2)
```

Next we add the command button.

```
myButton = QPushButton("OK")
myButton.clicked.connect(convert)
```

This button is on row 3, column 1, it spans 1 row and two columns.

```
layout.addWidget(myButton, 3, 1, 1, 2)
```

Finally, we need a function to deal with the inputs and convert the values. We can do this using an elif statement to match the values available in the conversions combo box.

```
def convert():
    if conversions.currentIndex() == 0:
        n = float(userInput.text()) * 0.39
        textLabel.setText(str(n))

    elif conversions.currentIndex() == 1:
        n = float(userInput.text()) * 2.54
        textLabel.setText(str(n))

    elif conversions.currentIndex() == 2:
        n = float(userInput.text()) * 0.62
        textLabel.setText(str(n))

    elif conversions.currentIndex() == 3:
        n = float(userInput.text()) * 1.60
        textLabel.setText(str(n))
```

The function will be called from myButton.clicked.connect(convert)

Once we write the code, we'll end up with something like this. You can select the conversions from the combo box, type in a number in the text box to convert, then click 'ok'.

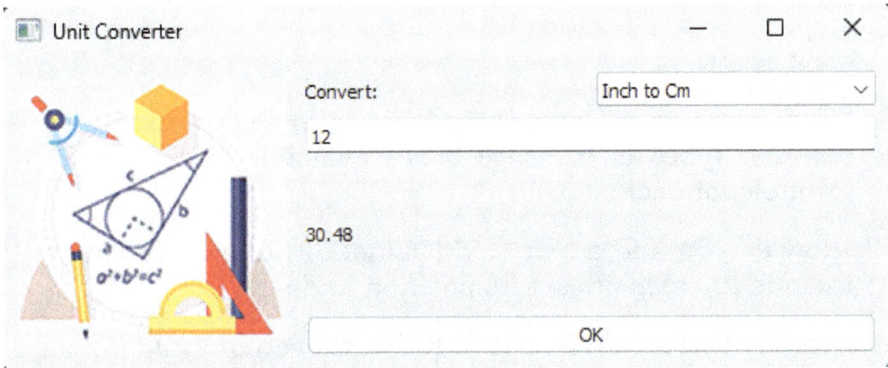

Lab Exercises 9.1

1. What is Tkinter and what is its role in Python programming?
2. How do you create a window in Tkinter? Explain the necessary steps with an example.
3. What are the different types of widgets available in Tkinter? Provide examples of each.
4. How do you handle button clicks in Tkinter? Explain with an example.
5. Explain the process of creating a menu bar in Tkinter. Include the steps required to add menu items and associate functions with them.
6. Design a basic paint program GUI using Tkinter. Include options for selecting different drawing tools (e.g., pencil, brush, shapes), colors, and line thickness. Allow the user to draw and save their artwork.
7. What are the necessary steps to create a window in PyQt? Explain each step briefly.
8. How can you add menus to a window in PyQt? Provide an example of creating a menu bar, menu, and menu items.

9. How do you display an image in PyQt? Explain the process and provide an example.

10. How do you add a button to a PyQt window? Include the steps to set its position, size, and connect a function to the click event.

11. How can you show message boxes in PyQt? Explain the different types of message boxes available and provide an example for each.

12. How do you add a text field (QLineEdit) to a PyQt window? Include the steps to set its position and size.

13. How do you create a list box (QListWidget) in PyQt? Explain how to add items to the list box and connect a function to handle item selection.

14. How do you add a checkbox (QCheckBox) to a PyQt window? Include the steps to set its position, size, and connect a function to handle state changes.

15. How do you add a label (QLabel) to a PyQt window? Explain the process and include the steps to set its position and size.

16. Create a simple file explorer application using PyQt. The application should display a list of files and folders in a specified directory and allow the user to navigate through the file system.

Summary

- Python libraries for creating graphics and GUIs include Tkinter, PyQt, and Kivy.
- Tkinter is a built-in Python library for creating simple GUI applications.
- PyQt is a cross-platform library for creating professional-looking GUI applications.
- Kivy is an open-source library for creating multitouch applications.
- Tkinter can be installed using the "pip install tk" command.
- To create a window in Tkinter, import the library, create an instance of the Tk class, and set properties such as title and geometry.
- Widgets such as menus, buttons, and text fields can be added to the window using Tkinter's built-in methods.
- The Canvas widget in Tkinter allows drawing shapes and images on the GUI.
- Message boxes can be created using the messagebox functions from the tkinter module.
- Input fields such as text fields and list boxes can be created using the Entry() and Listbox() functions, respectively.
- Checkboxes and labels can also be added to the GUI using the appropriate functions.
- PyQt is a more advanced library that provides extensive documentation and supports complex GUI applications.
- A simple calculator app can be created using Tkinter or PyQt by designing the interface and implementing the necessary logic for calculations.
- The main event loop, such as mainloop() in Tkinter, is used to run the GUI application and handle user interactions.

10 Turtle Graphics

Turtle graphics is a popular way of introducing programming concepts to beginners, particularly in the context of learning programming with Python. It is a concept that originated with the LOGO programming language developed in the late 1960s.

Turtle graphics provides a simple and intuitive way to create drawings and animations using a graphical turtle that can move, turn, and draw on a graphical canvas. The turtle can move forward or backward, turn left or right, and you can control its pen to draw lines as it moves.

For this chapter, you'll need to download the source code files from:

`elluminetpress.com/pytg`

You'll also find various video demos and tutorials.

The turtle is usually positioned at the center of the canvas, and by giving instructions, you can make the turtle move and draw shapes.

You can control the turtle by calling its methods. For example:

- forward()
- backward()
- left()
- right()
- penup()
- pendown()

Using these commands you can write programs to create various shapes, patterns, and designs, ranging from simple geometric figures to more complex artwork.

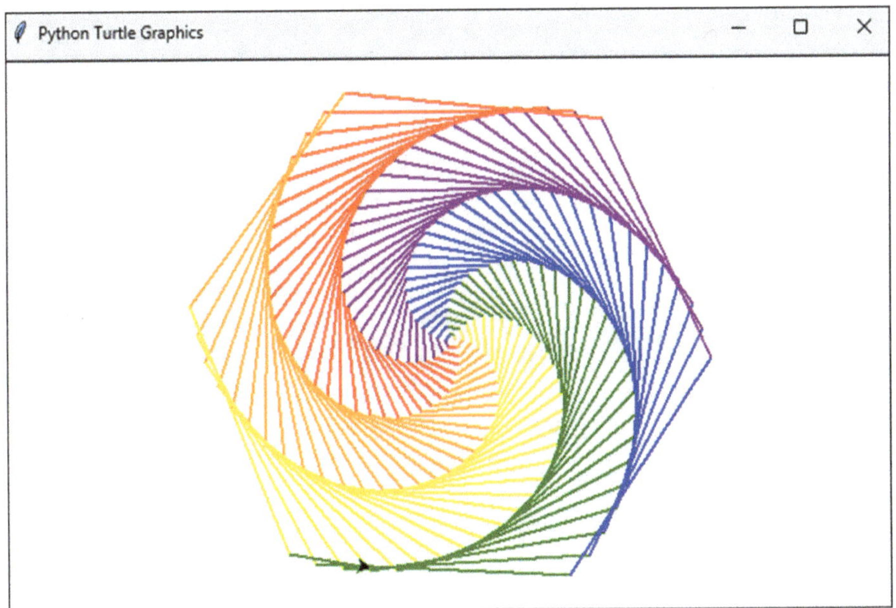

You can also change the turtle's appearance, such as its color and shape. The turtle object provides methods like color(), pensize(), or shape() to modify its attributes.

The Python includes a turtle module allowing you to create interesting drawings and animations using Python code.

Setting up Turtle Graphics

To start using the turtle, first you need to import the module

```
import turtle
```

Next, we need to create a turtle object

```
my_turtle = turtle.Turtle()
```

This will open a window with a turtle in the center. We can now draw some shapes.

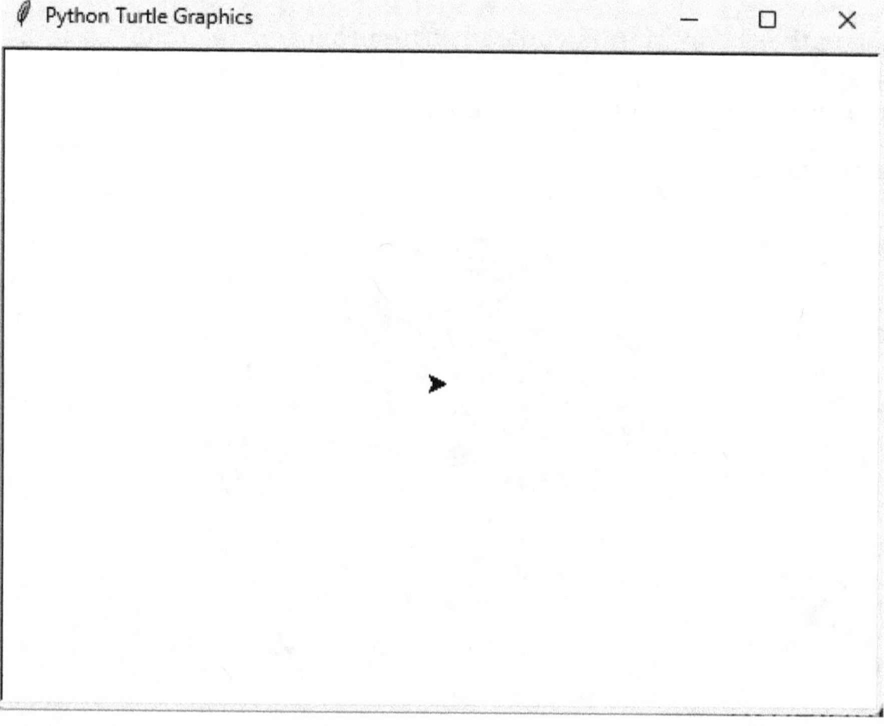

Basic Turtle Commands

The turtle module has some basic turtle commands that you can use to control and draw with the my_turtle object we created above.

In this case my_turtle is the object we created using the Turtle class defined in the turtle module.

Lets take a look at some commands

- **my_turtle.forward(distance)** moves the turtle forward in the current direction by the specified distance.
- **my_turtle.backward(distance)** moves the turtle backward in the opposite direction by the specified distance.
- **my_turtle.right(angle)** rotates the turtle's direction to the right by the specified angle (in degrees).
- **my_turtle.left(angle)** rotates the turtle's direction to the left by the specified angle (in degrees).
- **my_turtle.penup()** lifts the pen off the canvas, so the turtle can move without drawing.
- **my_turtle.pendown()** puts the pen down on the canvas, allowing the turtle to draw while moving.
- **my_turtle.pensize(width)** sets the width of the pen (line thickness) to the specified value.
- **my_turtle.pencolor(color)** sets the color of the pen to the specified color. Colors can be named strings (e.g., "red", "blue") or RGB tuples.
- **my_turtle.fillcolor(color)** sets the fill color for filled shapes, such as polygons or circles.
- **my_turtle.begin_fill()** marks the start of a shape to be filled with the fill color.
- **my_turtle.end_fill()** marks the end of a shape to be filled, and fills it with the specified color.
- **my_turtle.circle(radius)** draws a circle with the specified radius.
- **my_turtle.dot(size, color)** draws a dot with the specified size and color at the current turtle position.
- **my_turtle.setpos(x, y)** moves the turtle to the specified coordinates (x, y) on the canvas.
- **my_turtle.speed(speed)** sets the turtle's speed, where 1 is the slowest speed and 10 is the fastest.

Drawing Shapes & Patterns

We want to access the forward function, so we specify the module name it's in (turtle), followed by a dot, then the name of the function we want (forward). We can use

```
my_turtle.forward(100)
```

This will move the turtle 100 pixels forward.

You can also use to go backwards.

```
my_turtle.backward(100)
```

We can turn. For example, if we want to turn right 144 degrees.

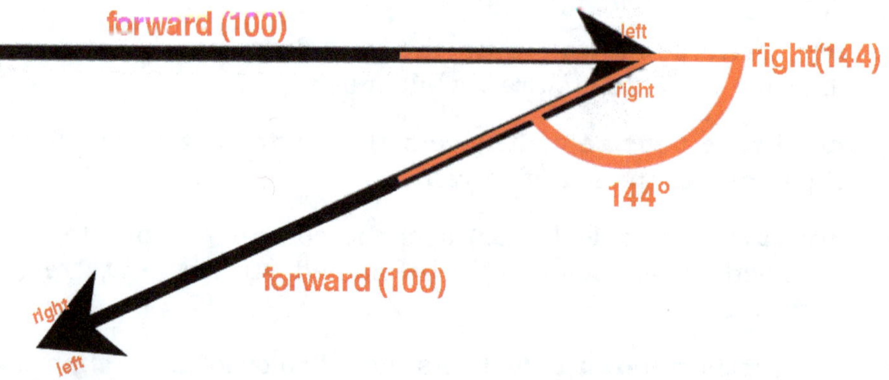

We use the following line.

```
my_turtle.right(144)
```

You can use loops to repeat commands to draw shapes. For example, if we wanted to draw a hexagon, we can use a for loop to repeat the commands for each side.

```
for sides in range(6):
    my_turtle.forward(100)
    my_turtle.right(60)
```

Or if you wanted to draw other shapes. How about a star?

```
for counter in range(5):
    myTurtle.right(144)
    myTurtle.forward(100)
```

Here, we moved the turtle 100 forward, then rotated the turtle 144 degrees to the right.

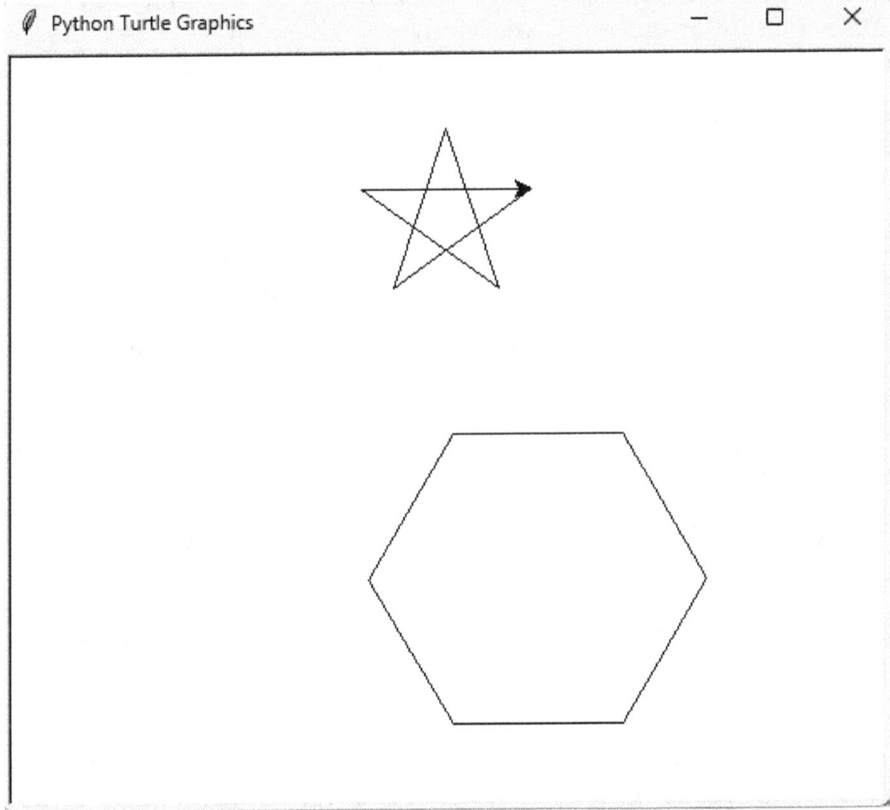

We can also start drawing patterns. Take a look at this example:

```
import turtle

my_turtle = turtle.Turtle()
my_screen = turtle.Screen()
for _ in range(36):

    for _ in range(2):
        my_turtle.forward(100)
        my_turtle.right(60)
        my_turtle.forward(100)
        my_turtle.right(120)
    my_turtle.right(10)

turtle.done()
```

First we import the turtle module then initialize the turtle and screen: The code creates a turtle object named my_turtle and a screen object named my_screen using the turtle.Turtle() and turtle.Screen() functions, respectively. These objects are used for drawing and managing the graphics.

We then enter the first for loop that executes 36 times. This loop is responsible for drawing the pattern multiple times.

Inside the main for loop, there is another loop that executes twice. This inner for loop is responsible for drawing a set of lines forming a shape. This is done with these commands

- my_turtle.forward(100) moves the turtle forward by 100 units.
- my_turtle.right(60) rotates the turtle to the right by 60 degrees.
- my_turtle.forward(100) moves the turtle forward by 100 units again.
- my_turtle.right(120) rotates the turtle to the right by 120 degrees.

After completing the inner loop, the code rotates the turtle to the right by 10 degrees using my_turtle.right(10). This ensures that each subsequent pattern is slightly rotated with respect to the previous one.

Try it out, have a look at flower.py

Lab Exercises 10.1

1. What is the purpose of creating a turtle object in turtle graphics?
2. What command can you use to move the turtle forward by a specified distance?
3. How would you rotate the turtle's direction to the right by a specified angle?
4. How can you lift the pen off the canvas so that the turtle can move without drawing?

5. How do you set the width of the pen (line thickness) in turtle graphics?
6. Write a program to draw a circle.
7. Write a program to draw a square.
8. Write a program to draw a triangle.

Summary

- Turtle graphics is a beginner-friendly way of learning programming concepts using Python.
- It originated from the LOGO programming language in the late 1960s.
- Turtle graphics allows you to create drawings and animations using a graphical turtle that can move, turn, and draw on a canvas.
- The turtle is positioned at the center of the canvas and can be controlled using commands.
- Basic turtle commands include moving forward and backward, rotating the turtle's direction, and lifting or putting down the pen.
- You can set the pen's width and color, fill shapes with colors, draw circles and dots, and control the turtle's speed.
- By combining these commands, you can create various shapes, patterns, and designs.
- To start using turtle graphics, import the turtle module and create a turtle object.
- The turtle object can then be used to call the available commands to draw on the canvas.
- Loops can be used to repeat commands and create complex shapes.
- Examples include drawing a square, triangle, circle, and star using the forward and right commands.

11 Game Development

Python offers a wide range of libraries and frameworks that make it easy to create games and handle various aspects of game development, such as graphics, physics, sound, and user input.

Pygame is suitable for developing 2D games and provides easy-to-use tools for handling sprites, animations, collision detection, and other common game development tasks. When it comes to 3D games, libraries like Panda3D offer more advanced features for rendering 3D models, handling lighting and shading, and managing complex scenes.

While Python may not be the best language for serious game development compared to C++, it makes an excellent choice for prototyping, learning game development concepts, and creating smaller-scale indie games.

For this chapter, you'll need to download the source code files from:

`elluminetpress.com/pygame`

You'll also find various video demos and tutorials.

Install Pygame

To install the module, open a command prompt. Make sure you run this as an administrator. On the command prompt type

```
pip install pygame
```

Once you press enter, the install will begin.

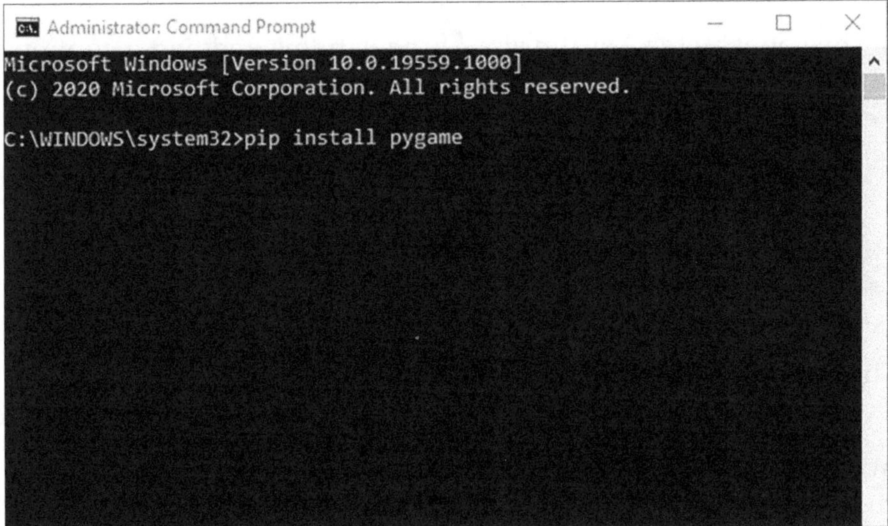

Allow the pip utility to download and install the module.

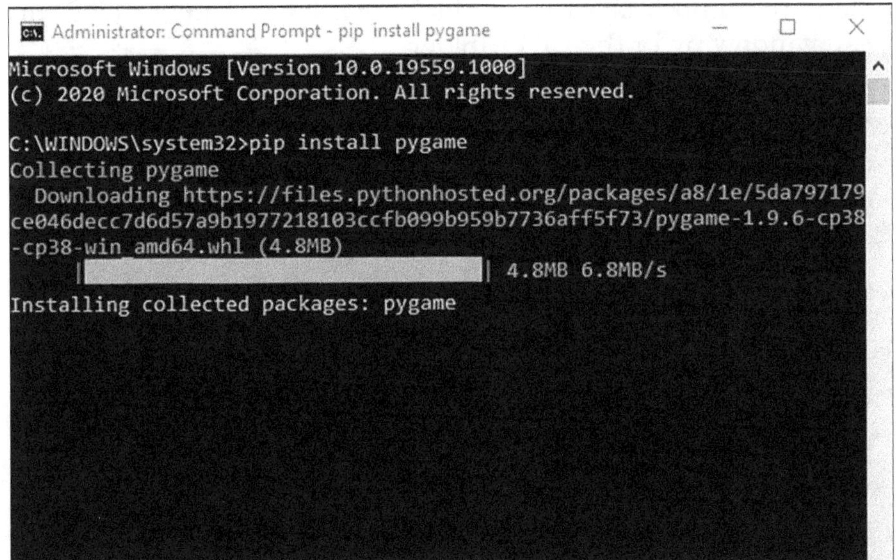

Creating a Window

To create a window for a game, first import the Pygame module

```
import pygame
```

Next, create a class to contain the game window

```
class GameWindow:
```

In the constructor, set the size of the window and add a caption to the title bar.

```
def __init__(self, width, height):
    self.width = width
    self.height = height
    self.screen = pygame.display.set_mode
                        ((self.width, self.height))
    pygame.display.set_caption("My Game")
```

The line self.screen creates the game window surface where you can draw various elements, including shapes, images, and text.

In the main program create an instance of the GameWindow class.

```
game = GameWindow(800, 600)
```

We should end up with a blank window. Take a look at createwindow.py in the Ch11 folder.

Setting up the Game Loop

The game loop is the part that controls the flow of a game. It is a continuous loop that runs throughout the entire duration of the game, handling various tasks such as updating the game state, rendering graphics, and processing user input.

We can add a run method to the GameWindow class. The code is as follows.

```
def run(self):
    running = True
    while running:
        for event in pygame.event.get():
            if event.type == pygame.QUIT:
                running = False
        pygame.display.flip()

    pygame.quit()
```

In the main program we can call the game loop

```
game.run()
```

Take a look at gameloop.py in the Ch11 folder.

The variable 'running' indicates whether the game is running or not. We initially set it to True, indicating that the program is running.

The while loop continues until 'running' is set to False. This is the main game loop

Within the while loop, we use a for loop to iterate over the events that have occurred since the last iteration. The if statement checks if the event type is pygame.QUIT, which represents the user trying to close the game window. If the event type is pygame.QUIT, we set the running variable to False, which will break out of the while loop and terminate the program.

After the for loop, we call pygame.display.flip() to update the game display.

Finally, after exiting the while loop, we call pygame.quit() to properly clean up and close the Pygame modules and resources.

Drawing Basic Shapes

To draw shapes, use the draw function.

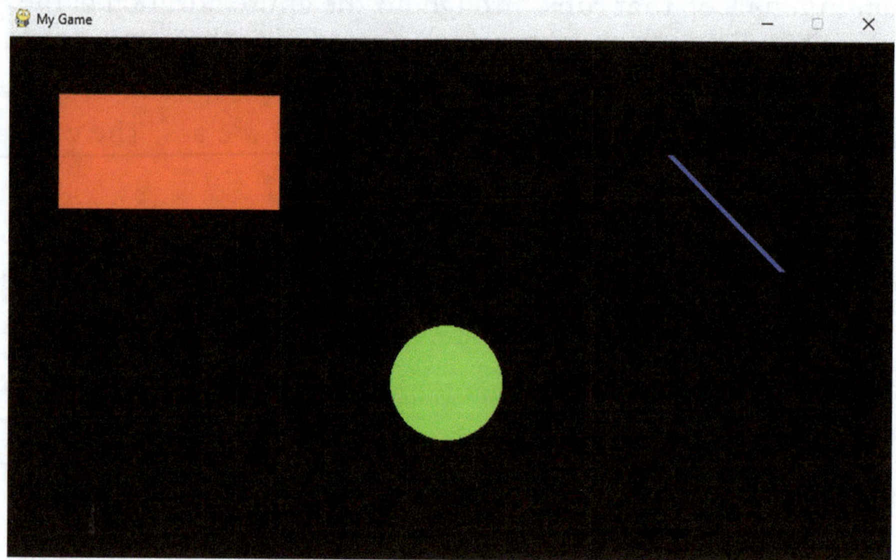

Square

We can draw a square using the following:

```
pygame.draw.rect(self.screen, (255,0,0),
                              (50,50,200,100))
```

The first parameter self.screen is the surface on which the rectangle will be drawn.

In this case, it's self.screen that represents the game window surface stored within the GameWindow class.

The second parameter (255, 0, 0) is the color of the rectangle specified as an RGB tuple. In this example, (255, 0, 0) represents red, as it has maximum red intensity (255) and no green or blue intensity (0).

The third parameter (50, 50, 200, 100) is the position and size of the rectangle specified as (x, y, width, height). In this case, the rectangle's top-left corner is positioned at (50, 50), and it has a width of 200 pixels and a height of 100 pixels.

Circle

We can draw a circle using the following:

```
pygame.draw.circle(self.screen, (0,255,0),
                                (400,300),
                                 50)
```

The first parameter self.screen is the surface on which the circle will be drawn. In this case, it's self.screen that represents the game window surface stored within the GameWindow class.

The second parameter (0, 255, 0) is the color of the circle specified as an RGB tuple. In this example, (0, 255, 0) represents green, as it has no red intensity (0), maximum green intensity (255), and no blue intensity (0).

The third parameter (400, 300) is the center position of the circle specified as (x, y). In this case, the circle's center is positioned at (400, 300).

The fourth parameter (50) is the radius of the circle. In this example, the radius is set to 50 pixels.

Line

We can draw a line using the following:

```
pygame.draw.line(self.screen, (0,0,255),
                              (600,100),
                              (700,200),
                               5)
```

The first parameter self.screen is the surface on which the line will be drawn.

In this case, self.screen represents the game window surface stored within the GameWindow class.

The second parameter (0, 0, 255) is the color of the line specified as an RGB tuple. In this example, (0, 0, 255) represents blue, as it has no red intensity (0), no green intensity (0), and maximum blue intensity (255).

The third parameter (600, 100) is the starting point of the line specified as (x, y). In this case, the line starts at the coordinates (600, 100).

The fourth parameter (700, 200) is the ending point of the line specified as (x, y). In this example, the line ends at the coordinates (700, 200).

The fifth parameter (5) is the width of the line. In this case, the line has a width of 5 pixels.

Take a look at addshapes.py in the Ch11 folder.

Loading Images

To load an image, we use the load() function. We can add this to the constructor __init__ method of our GameWindow class to load the image

```
self.image = pygame.image.load("rocket.png")
```

Next we need to create a rectangle object that represents the dimensions and position of the loaded image. This rectangle object is useful for various purposes, including collision detection, positioning, and blitting the image onto the game window.

```
self.image_rect = self.image.get_rect()
```

Set the initial position of the image.

```
self.image_rect.center = (self.width // 2,
                          self.height // 2)
```

Inside the game loop run method, we need to send the image to the screen. We can do this using the blit function.

```
self.screen.blit(self.image, self.image_rect)
```

The first part of the line self.screen refers to the Pygame surface object representing the game window. The blit() function is called on this surface to draw the image onto it.

self.image represents the image that you loaded using pygame.image.load() and stored in the self.image attribute. This is the image that will be drawn on the game window.

self.image_rect is a rectangle object that represents the position and dimensions of the image. The blit() function uses the self.image_rect object to determine where the image should be drawn on the game window. The self.image_rect object stores the current position of the image.

Have a look at addimage.py in the Ch11 folder

Keyboard Events

To add key controls to move the image in the game window, we need to update the game loop.

In the run method of our GameWindow class, we can add an elif statement to handle the input from the cursor keys on the keyboard.

First, we need to check for key presses. We can do this with an if statement

```
if event.type == pygame.KEYDOWN:
```

Then in the elif statement, we create a case for each of the four keys: left, right, up, down.

```
    if event.key == pygame.K_LEFT:
        self.image_rect.x -= 10

    elif event.key == pygame.K_RIGHT:
        self.image_rect.x += 10

    elif event.key == pygame.K_UP:
        self.image_rect.y -= 10

    elif event.key == pygame.K_DOWN:
        self.image_rect.y += 10
```

To move the image up we update the x coordinate of our image.rect that contains the image of the rocket.

The x and y values move the top left corner of the rectangle.

To move it to the left, we reduce the x value.

To move it up we reduce the y value as we can see in on page 178.

Similarly going the other way. To move the image down, we increase the y value, to move it right we increase the x value, as we can see in the figure below.

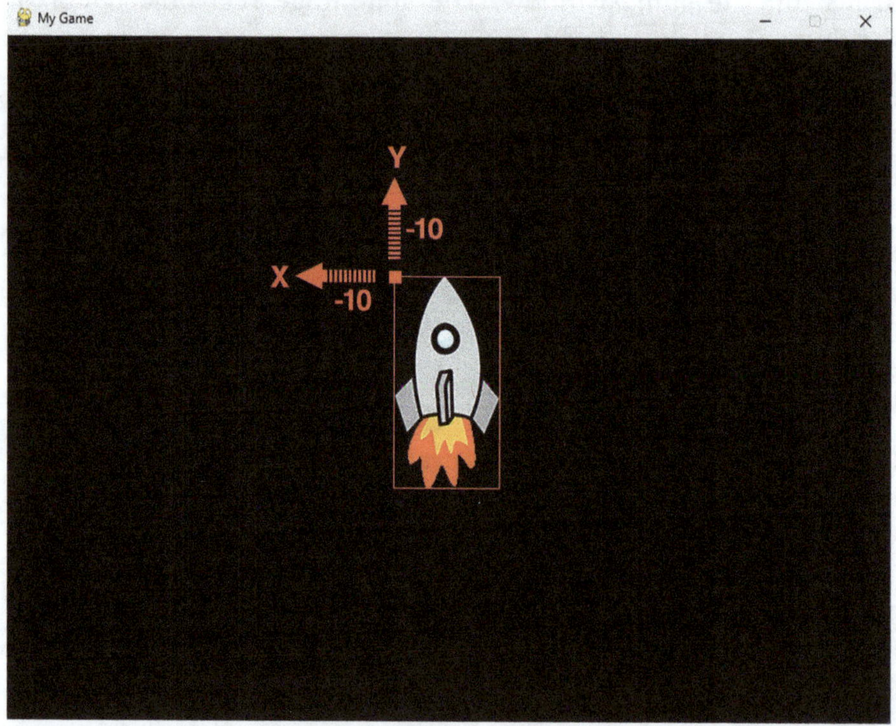

Finally we need to clear the screen before we blit the rocket in its new position. We add the following code just before blit.

```
self.screen.fill((0, 0, 0))
```

Otherwise, we'll end up with this.

Have a look at keyboardevents.py in the Ch11 folder.

Sprites & Animation

A sprite is a graphical representation of a game object or character that can be moved, animated, and interacted with within the game world. Sprites are typically 2D images or animations that are rendered onto the game screen.

Creating a Simple Animation

Animation in Pygame involves displaying a series of images (or frames) in a rapid sequence to create the illusion of motion.

To create an animation, you need a series of images. These frames can be loaded from an image file such as PNG using the pygame.image.load() function. You can load the frames individually or from a directory using functions like os.listdir() to iterate over the files. If you have lots of frames it makes sense to load them from a directory. To keep things simple, we are going to load three frames individually so you can see how the process works. The following loads the png images and places them in a list called image_sprite..

```
image_sprite = [pygame.image.load("frame01.png"),
                pygame.image.load("frame02.png"),
                pygame.image.load("frame03.png")]
```

Now, inside the game loop we set the frame rate using the clock. tick function. This makes sure the program runs at a reasonable speed.

```
clock = pygame.time.Clock()
```

Next, we add a counter to count each frame.

```
frame = 0
```

All you need to do now is to show each image in the image_sprite list at a time. Since we want to show the three frames over and over again, we need to reset the frame counter back to 0 when we get to the end of the image_sprite list. We can check for the end of the list by using the following.

```
if value >= len(image_sprite):
    value = 0
```

Before displaying the first frame, we want to clear the screen to remove any previous frames. In this example, we just fill the screen with white, but this could also be a background image.

```
window.fill((255, 255, 255))
```

After that, we want to display the current frame. Here in the blit function, we're passing the current frame in the image_sprite list, followed by the x and y position where we want the image to appear on the screen.

```
window.blit(image_sprite[frame], (0, 140))
```

Finally, we update the display and increment the frame counter

```
pygame.display.update()
frame += 1
```

Have a look at sprite.py in the Ch11 folder. Make sure you also have the files frame01.png, frame02.png, and frame03.png in the same folder.

If there are a lot of frames, we can load the frames into the list using a loop. For example.

First assign the string "ufo_frames" to the variable frames_directory. This is the directory where the frames are saved.

```
frames_directory = "ufo_frames"
```

Retrieve a list of filenames within the directory.

```
frame_filenames = os.listdir(frames_directory)
```

Create an empty list to store the frames

```
image_sprite = []
```

Using a for loop we iterate over each file in the frame_filenames directory

```
for filename in frame_filenames:
```

Inside the for loop, we check if the current filename ends with the extension ".png". It ensures that only PNG files are considered for loading as frame images.

```
if filename.endswith(".png"):
```

The pygame.image.load function loads the image file located in the frames_directory with the given filename.

```
image = pygame.image.load
        (os.path.join(frames_directory, filename))
```

Finally add the image to the image_sprite list.

```
        image_sprite.append(image)
```

Take a look at sprite2.py in the Ch11 folder.

Music

Pygame supports several audio formats for music, such as MP3, WAV, Midi, OGG, and MOD.

To add audio using Pygame, you'll need to load an audio file

```
pygame.mixer.music.load('path/to/audio/file.mp3')
```

To play the audio use play()

```
pygame.mixer.music.play()
```

To control the playback, use the functions like pause(), unpause() and stop(). For example:

```
pygame.mixer.music.pause()      # Pause the audio
pygame.mixer.music.unpause()    # Unpause the audio
pygame.mixer.music.stop()       # Stop the audio
```

You can also set the volume of the audio using the `set_volume()` function, which takes a value between 0.0 and 1.0:

```
pygame.mixer.music.set_volume(0.5)  # Set vol to 50%
```

To ensure that the audio continues playing, you can add a loop:

```
while pygame.mixer.music.get_busy():
    pygame.time.Clock().tick(10
```

Let's take a look at an example. Have a look at audio1.py in the Ch11 folder.

```
import pygame

pygame.init()

pygame.mixer.music.load('music.mp3')
pygame.mixer.music.play()

while pygame.mixer.music.get_busy():
    pygame.time.Clock().tick(10)

pygame.mixer.music.stop()

pygame.quit()
```

Sound Effects

Pygame supports playing sound effects in addition to music. Sound effects are typically short audio clips used for in-game actions like explosions, footsteps, or button clicks.

Here's an example of how to play a sound effect using Pygame:

To add sound effects in Pygame,first load the sound effect file:

```
sound_effect = pygame.mixer.Sound('laser.mp3')
```

To play the sound effect:

```
sound_effect.play()
```

By default, the sound effect will play once. If you want to repeat the sound effect, you can use the play() function in a loop.

To adjust the sound effect volume. The `set_volume()` function allows you to adjust the volume of the sound effect. It takes a value between 0.0 and 1.0, where 0.0 is mute and 1.0 is full volume.

```
sound_effect.set_volume(0.5)
```

To ensure that the audio continues playing, you can add a loop:

```
while pygame.mixer.music.get_busy():
    pygame.time.Clock().tick(10)
```

Let's take a look at an example. Have a look at audio2.py in the Ch11 folder.

```
import pygame

pygame.mixer.init()
sound_effect = pygame.mixer.Sound("laser.mp3")
sound_effect.play()

while pygame.mixer.get_busy():
    pygame.time.Clock().tick(10)

pygame.mixer.quit()
```

Invaders Project

We are going to build a simple game using the techniques we learned above with object-oriented programming principles we learned in chapter 7.

The objective of the project is to control a rocket to shoot down UFOs using bullets while avoiding bombs dropped from the UFOs.

Specification

This is how the game should work.

1. Rocket (player):

    - The rocket should be displayed as an image on the screen.
    - It should start at the bottom center of the screen.
    - If the rocket collides with a UFO's bomb, the rocket should explode and reset to its initial position.

2. UFOs (enemy):

    - UFOs should be displayed as animated sprites on the screen.
    - UFOs should move horizontally across the screen, bouncing off the edges.
    - Each UFO should drop bombs periodically towards the rocket.
    - If a UFO is hit by a bullet, it should explode and respawn at a random position on the screen.

3. Bullets:

    - The rocket should be able to shoot bullets to destroy UFOs.
    - The bullets should be displayed as images on the screen.

- When a bullet collides with a UFO, the UFO should explode.
- The bullets should move vertically upward from the rocket's position.
- If a bullet goes off-screen, it should reset to the rocket's position.

4. Collision Detection:
    - Collision detection should be implemented between the rocket and UFOs' bombs.
    - Collision detection should be implemented between the bullets and UFOs.
5. Explosions:
    - Explosions should be displayed on the screen when a UFO or the rocket is hit.
    - The explosions should be shown using explosion images.
6. User Interface:
    - The game should have a window with a resolution of 800x600 pixels.
    - The game window should have a title displaying "My Invaders".
    - The background of the game window should be displayed as an image.
    - The rocket, UFOs, bullets, and explosions should be displayed on top of the background.
7. Controls:
    - The rocket should be controlled using the left and right arrow keys, but not up or down.
    - The spacebar should be used to fire bullets from the rocket.

8. Game Loop:

    - The game loop should continuously update the positions of the rocket, UFOs, bombs, and bullets.
    - The game loop should render the updated positions and images on the screen.
    - The game loop should run at a fixed frame rate of 25 frames per second.

Building the Application

Here, we're going to start building the application specified above. Let's start with creating a window.

So you can understand the process of building the game, I'm going to go through it step by step. I have included the source code in the Ch11 folder so you can study the code and execute it using the python interpreter.

Let's begin...

Initialise and Create Window

The first thing we're going to build is the user interface. Have a look at project01.py

Import the necessary Pygame module, then initializes.

```
import pygame
pygame.init()
```

Create a game window 800x600 pixels and set the window title.

```
screen = pygame.display.set_mode((800, 600))
pygame.display.set_caption("My Invaders")
```

Load the background image and assign to background variable.

```
background = pygame.image.load("bg.jpg")
```

Create a game clock. This will be used to control the frame rate of the game.

```
clock = pygame.time.Clock()
```

Create Program or Game Loop

The game loop is a continuous loop that controls the flow of the game and ensures that the game is updated, rendered, and events are handled in a consistent manner. This usually involves processing user input, update positions of sprites and objects, render the objects or sprites on the screen, and updating the display. We can do this with a while loop

```
running = True
while running:
```

Set the clock to control the frame rate of the game.

```
clock.tick(25)
```

Next, we need to clear the screen to draw the updated sprites and objects on the screen. In this case we fill the screen with the background image using the blit funciton.

```
screen.blit(background, (0, 0))
```

The updated screen is displayed using pygame.display.update() function.

```
pygame.display.update()
```

The game loop continues until the running variable is set to False, which can happen when the user closes the game window.

Add the Player

The first object we want to add is the rocket ship for the player to control. To do this we first create a class for our rocket. Have a look at project02.py

```
class Rocket:
    def __init__(self, screen):
        self.screen = screen
        self.image = pygame.image.load("rocket.png")
        self.image = pygame.transform.scale(
                                    self.image, (50, 100))
        self.rect = self.image.get_rect()
        self.rect.centerx = screen.get_rect().centerx
        self.rect.bottom = screen.get_rect().bottom
```

Let's take a look at what the code does.

self.screen assigns the screen parameter to the self.screen attribute. This line stores the reference to the Pygame screen surface in the Rocket object.

self.image = pygame.image.load("rocket.png") loads the rocket image from the file "rocket.png" using pygame.image.load(). It assigns the loaded image to the self.image attribute.

self.image = pygame.transform.scale(self.image, (50, 100)) resizes the rocket image to a width of 50 pixels and a height of 100 pixels using pygame.transform.scale() and updates the self.image attribute with the resized image.

self.rect = self.image.get_rect() creates a rectangle (self.rect) based on the dimensions of the rocket image using self.image.get_rect(). The rectangle represents the boundaries of the rocket's image.

self.rect.centerx = screen.get_rect().centerx sets the center x-coordinate of the rocket's rectangle to the center x-coordinate of the screen surface using self.rect.centerx = screen.get_rect().centerx. This positions the rocket horizontally at the center of the screen.

self.rect.bottom = screen.get_rect().bottom sets the bottom y-coordinate of the rocket's rectangle to the bottom y-coordinate of the screen surface using self.rect.bottom = screen.get_rect().bottom. This positions the rocket vertically at the bottom of the screen.

Now we need a method to draw the rocket on the screen.

```
def draw(self):
    self.screen.blit(self.image, self.rect)
```

We also want the rocket ship to be able to move, so we can add two other methods

```
def move_left(self):
    self.rect.centerx -= 10

def move_right(self):
    self.rect.centerx += 10
```

In the main program, we can create a rocket object from this class

```
rocket = Rocket(screen)
```

Next, in the game loop, we want to draw the rocket on the screen.

```
    rocket.draw()
```

Add Keyboard Controls

To add keyboard controls so the player can move the rocket ship. Now, we need to create an event handler in the game loop. Have a look at project03.py.

Using a for loop, we can use pygame.event.get() to retrieve a list of all the events that have occurred since the last time this line was called.

```
    for event in pygame.event.get():
```

Inside the for loop, we can check for events. We do this using an elif statement. If the event type is pygame.QUIT, this means the user has clicked the close button on the game window. In this case, the running variable is set to False which breaks out of the game loop and terminates the game.

```
        if event.type == pygame.QUIT:
            running = False
```

If the user hasn't clicked the close button, we check to see what key has been pressed.

If the event type is pygame.KEYDOWN, it means the user has pressed a key on the keyboard. If this is the case, then we need to check which key has been pressed. We do this with another elif statement.

```
        elif event.type == pygame.KEYDOWN:
```

If the left arrow key (pygame.K_LEFT) is pressed, the rocket.move_left() method is called, which moves the rocket to the left.

```
            if event.key == pygame.K_LEFT:
                rocket.move_left()
```

If the right arrow key (pygame.K_RIGHT) is pressed, the rocket. move_right() method is called, which moves the rocket to the right.

```
            elif event.key == pygame.K_RIGHT:
                rocket.move_right()
```

Now when you run the program, you can move the rocket ship left and right.

Making the Rocket Fire Bullets

To make the rocket fire bullets, first we need to create a new class to represent a bullet. Have a look at project04.py

```
class Bullet:
    def __init__(self, screen, rocket):
        self.screen = screen
        self.image = pygame.image.load("bullet.png")
        self.rect = self.image.get_rect()
        self.rect.centerx = rocket.rect.centerx
        self.rect.bottom = rocket.rect.top
```

We'll also need a method to draw the bullet on the screen

```
    def draw(self):
        self.screen.blit(self.image, self.rect)
```

Another method to move the bullet up the screen.

```
    def move(self):
        self.rect.y -= 10
```

After we have our new Bullet class, we need to create a bullet object in the main program

```
bullet = Bullet(screen, rocket)
bullet_state = "ready"
```

Next, we need to add an option to the event handler loop to configure what happens when we press the space bar. According to the specification this is to fire bullets from the rocket.

To the keydown events, we just add another elif statement to configure what happens when the spacebar is pressed.

```
elif event.key == pygame.K_SPACE:
    if bullet_state == "ready":
        bullet_state = "fire"
        bullet.rect.centerx = rocket.rect.centerx
        bullet.rect.bottom = rocket.rect.top
```

After we have moved the rocket, we need to move and redraw the bullet if it is fired (if the player presses space). If the bullet gets to the top of the screen (ie < 0) we can stop moving and redrawing the bullet on screen.

```
if bullet_state == "fire":
    bullet.move()
    bullet.draw()
    if bullet.rect.bottom < 0:
        bullet_state = "ready"
```

Study the code in project04.py in the Ch11 folder. Now you will be able to fire a bullet from the rocket ship.

Add Enemies to Shoot

Now that we have created our rocket for the player to control, we need to add some enemies (UFOs) for the player to shoot. Have a look at project05.py

```
class UFO:
    def __init__(self, screen):
        self.screen = screen
        self.image = pygame.image.load("ufo.png")
        self.image = pygame.transform.scale
                            (self.image, (70, 50))
        self.rect = self.image.get_rect()
        self.reset_position()

    def draw(self):
        self.screen.blit(self.image, self.rect)

    def reset_position(self):
        self.rect.x = random.randint(0, self.screen.
                      get_width() - self.rect.width)
        self.rect.y = random.randint(0, self.screen.
              get_height() // 2 - self.rect.height)
```

Create a UFO object in the main program

```
ufo = UFO(screen)
```

Draw the ufo object in the game loop

```
ufo.draw()
```

Collision Detection

When you fire the bullet from the rocket, you'll notice that it flies straight past the ufo. In the game we want the bullet to destroy the ufo. To do this we need to use collision detection. We can do this colliderect() method provided by the pygame.Rect class. This method checks whether two rectangles overlap or intersect with each other.

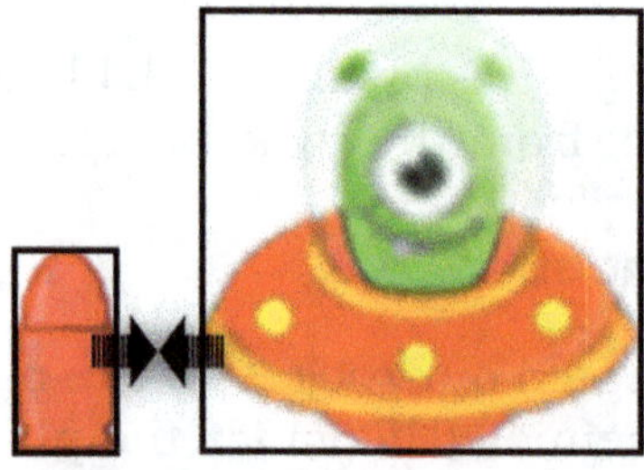

In the game loop, we can check for a collision between the bullet and the UFO using the following condition:

```
if bullet_state == "fire" and bullet.rect.
colliderect(ufo.rect):
    bullet_state = "ready"
    ufo.reset_position()
```

The condition bullet_state == "fire" ensures that the bullet is in motion before checking for a collision. If the bullet is not fired (bullet_state == "ready"), the collision check is skipped.

The line bullet.rect.colliderect(ufo.rect) checks if the rectangles containing the bullet and the UFO intersect. If they do intersect, it means a collision has occurred. If a collision is detected, the bullet is reset to the "ready" state (bullet_state = "ready") so that it can be fired again. The UFO's position is also reset using the reset_position() method to make it appear in a new random position.

What happens if the UFO is hit? We can add an explosion image to show this. To do this, we'll need to modify the UFO class init method to load the explosion image and add it to a rectangle

```
def __init__(self, screen):
    self.screen = screen
    self.image = pygame.image.load("ufo.png")
    self.image = pygame.transform.scale(self.image,
                                        (70, 50))
    self.rect = self.image.get_rect()
    self.reset_position()
    self.explosion_image = pygame.image.load
                           ("explosion.png")
    self.explosion_image = pygame.transform.scale
                           (self.explosion_image,
                           (70, 70))
    self.explosion_rect = self.explosion_image.get_rect()
    self.explosion_timer = 0
```

We'll also need to modify the draw method to draw the explosion when the UFO is hit.

```
def draw(self):
    if self.explosion_timer > 0:
        self.screen.blit(self.explosion_image,
                         self.explosion_rect)
        self.explosion_timer -= 1
    else:
        self.screen.blit(self.image, self.rect)
```

We can also add a line to explode the UFO in the collision detection in the game loop. Have a look at project06.py in the Ch11 folder.

Make the UFOs Move

Have a look at project08.py. To make the UFOs move, we need to add a method to the UFO class to move and update the position of the UFO on screen. To do this we can simply change the x and y positions of the rectangle containing the UFO image.

```
def update(self):
    self.rect.x += self.speed_x
    self.rect.y += self.speed_y
```

In this method, we'll also need to make sure the UFO doesn't go off the edges of the screen. We can do this with a simple if statement. If UFO hits left edge or right edge, reverse direction.

```
if self.rect.left <=0 or self.rect.right >= self.
screen.get_width():
    self.speed_x *= -1
```

Similarly for top and bottom edge.

```
if self.rect.top <=0 or self.rect.bottom >= self.
screen.get_height():
    self.speed_y *= -1
```

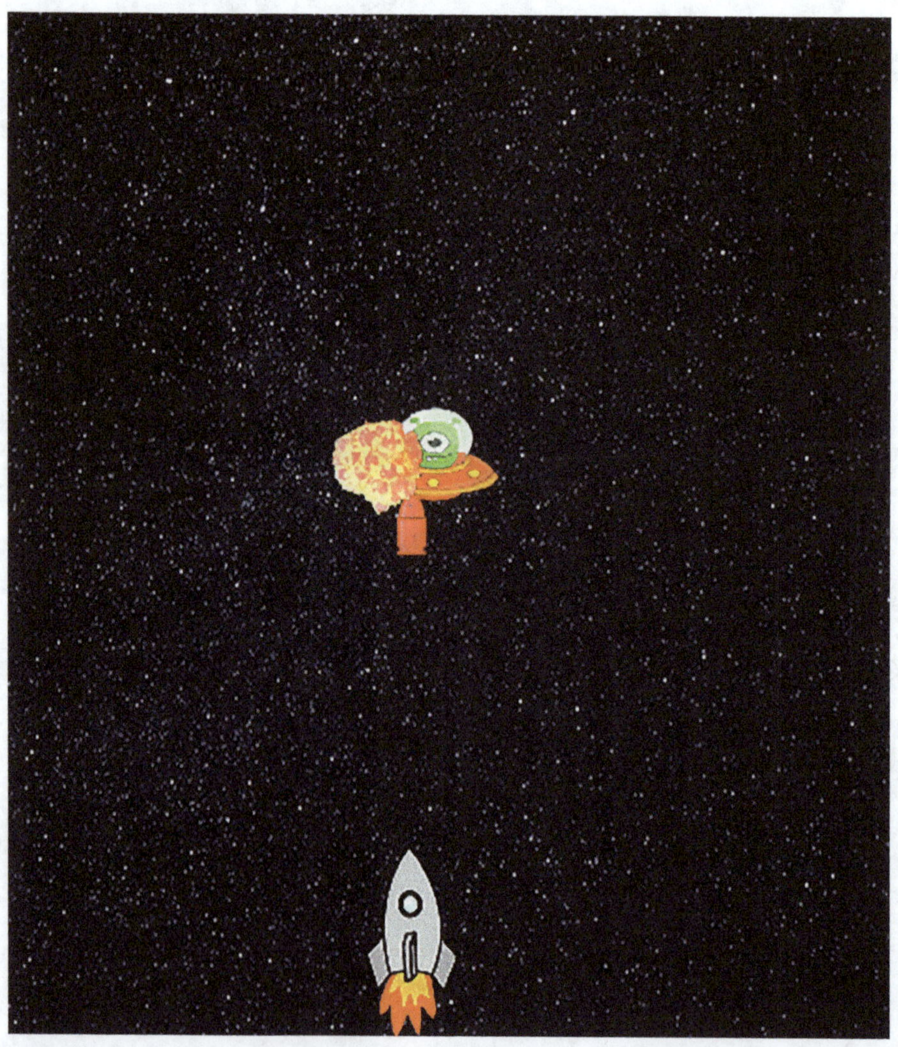

Make the UFOs Drop Bombs

To make the UFO drop bombs, first we need to create a class to represent a bomb. Have a look at project09.py

```
class Bomb:
    def __init__(self, screen, ufo):
        self.screen = screen
        self.image = pygame.image.load("bomb.png")
        self.rect = self.image.get_rect()
        self.rect.centerx = ufo.rect.centerx
        self.rect.top = ufo.rect.bottom

    def draw(self):
        self.screen.blit(self.image, self.rect)

    def move(self):
        self.rect.y += 5
```

Next we need to update the UFO class to drop a bomb. To do this we need to add a drop_bomb method

```
    def drop_bomb(self):
        bomb = Bomb(self.screen, self)
        bombs.append(bomb)
```

We'll also need to modify the method to update the position of the bombs

```
        if self.bomb_timer <= 0:
            self.drop_bomb()
            self.bomb_timer = self.bomb_interval
        else:
            self.bomb_timer -= 1
```

We need to add methods to the rocket class to determine what to do when the rocket explodes.

```
    def explode(self):
       self.explosion_rect.center = self.rect.center
       self.explosion_timer = 10
```

Here we reset the position of the rocket back to the middle of the screen. We set the explosion timer to display the explosion image for 10 frames.

In the game loop we can add a section to update the bombs position.

```
for bomb in bombs:
    bomb.move()
    bomb.draw()
    if bomb.rect.colliderect(rocket.rect):
        rocket_hit = True
        break
    if bomb.rect.top > screen.get_height():
        bombs.remove(bomb)
```

Then check for a collision between the rocket and the bomb

```
if rocket_hit:
    rocket.explode()
    rocket.reset_position()
    rocket_hit = False
```

Breakout Project

Breakout is a classic arcade game that was released by Atari in 1976. The objective of the game is to break a wall of bricks by bouncing a ball off a paddle. The player controls the paddle at the bottom of the screen.

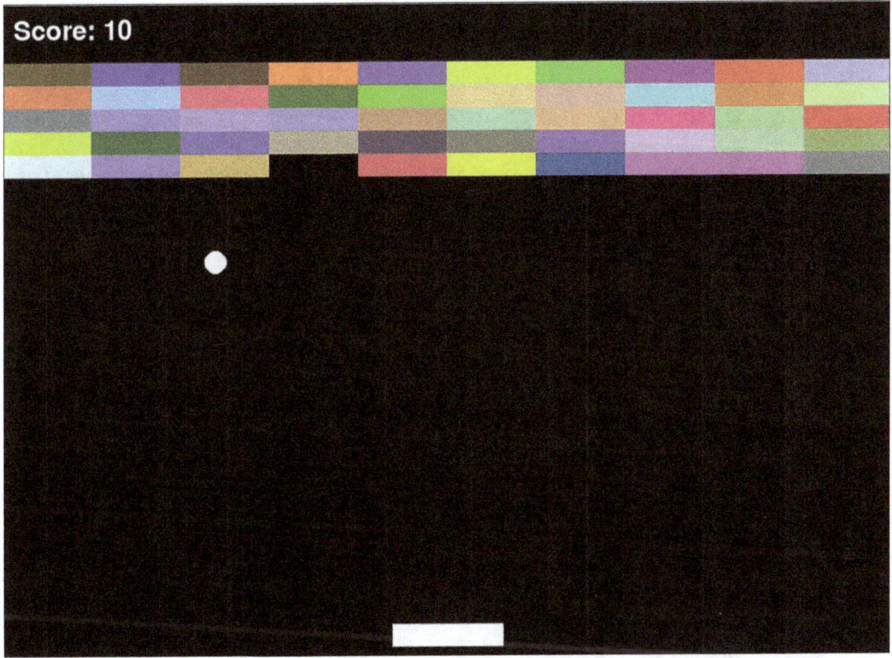

Using what you've learned in this chapter, write an object oriented program to create the game. The game will need to function as follows.

Game Window: A window is displayed where the game is played. The window has a fixed size of 800x600 pixels.

Paddle: The player controls a paddle at the bottom of the screen using the left and right arrow keys. The paddle moves horizontally to hit the ball.

Ball: A ball starts at the center of the screen and moves in a diagonal direction. It bounces off the walls, paddle, and bricks.

Bricks: Arranged in a grid pattern at the top of the screen. The player's goal is to break all the bricks by hitting them with the ball.

Collision Detection: The game checks for collisions between the ball and the walls, paddle, and bricks. When a collision occurs, appropriate actions are taken (e.g., bouncing off, destroying bricks).

Score: The player earns points for each brick they break. The score is displayed on the screen.

Game Over: The game ends when either the ball falls off the bottom of the screen or all bricks are destroyed. The final score is shown, and a "Game Over" message is displayed.

Build the program. Here is the pseudo code of how the program should be written.

```
Initialize pygame
Create the game window
Set the title of the game window
Create a clock object for frame rate control
Create a font object for rendering text

Define a Paddle class
    Initialize the paddle object
    Set the initial position and size of the paddle

Define a Ball class
    Initialize the ball object
    Set the initial position, size, and speed of ball
    Update the ball position based on speed
    Handle collisions with walls, paddle & bricks

Define a Brick class
    Initialize a brick object with position & color

Create the paddle object
Create the ball object
Create a group to hold the bricks

Create bricks by iterating over rows and columns
    Calculate the position of each brick
    Choose a random color for each brick
    Create a brick object with the calculated
    position and chosen color
    Add the brick to the group of bricks
```

```
Create a group to hold all sprites
Add the paddle, ball, and bricks to the group of
sprites

Initialize the score and game_over variables

Set key repetition delay and interval

Game loop
    Handle events (e.g., window close, key presses)
    Update all sprites and check for game over
    Clear the screen
    Draw all sprites on the window
    Render and display the score text
    Update the window
    Limit the frame rate

Display "Game Over" text
```

Have a look at breakoutstarter.py. See if you can write the program. If you get stuck have a look at breakoutfinal.py and study the code. I have included comments to explain what each line does.

breakoutstarter.py - D:\OneDrive\Elluminet Press\Production\Program...

File Edit Format Run Options Window Help

```
import pygame
import random

# Initialize pygame
pygame.init()

# Create the game window
window_width = 800
window_height = 600
window = pygame.display.set_mode((window_width, window_height))

# Set the title of the game window
pygame.display.set_caption("Brick Breaker")

# Create a clock object for frame rate control
clock = pygame.time.Clock()

# Create a font object for rendering text
font = pygame.font.Font(None, 36)
```

Lab Exercises 11.1

1. Explain the concept of surfaces in Pygame and how they are used for drawing and manipulating graphics?

2. How can you manipulate and transform surfaces in Pygame, such as scaling, rotating, or flipping them?

3. What are some strategies for efficiently rendering and updating game surfaces in Pygame to ensure smooth gameplay and optimal performance?

4. Write a Pygame program that displays a window with a given width and height. Set the window title and fill the window with a specific background color.

5. Write program that displays a shape (e.g., a rectangle or circle) in the center of the window.

6. Implement keyboard input so that when the arrow keys are pressed, the shape you created in exercise 5 moves in the corresponding direction.

7. What are sprites in Pygame, and how can they be used to create animated objects?

8. How do you load and display images using Pygame?

9. How can you implement collision detection between game surfaces in Pygame to handle interactions between game objects?

Summary

- Python offers libraries and frameworks for game development, such as Pygame for 2D games and Panda3D for 3D games.
- Pygame is cross-platform and allows you to create games that run on different operating systems.
- To install Pygame, use the command "pip install pygame" in the command prompt.
- Creating a game window involves importing the Pygame module and defining a class with the window size and caption.
- The game loop controls the flow of the game and handles tasks like updating the game state and processing user input.
- Pygame provides functions for drawing basic shapes like squares, circles, and lines.
- Images can be loaded using the Pygame "image.load()" function and displayed on the game window using the "blit()" function.
- Keyboard events can be handled to control game elements like moving an image on the screen.
- Sprites and animations can be created by displaying a series of images in a rapid sequence.
- Pygame supports playing music and sound effects in various audio formats.
- While Pygame itself doesn't include a built-in physics engine, you can integrate popular physics libraries such as Pygame Physics Engine (Pymunk) or Box2D to incorporate realistic physics simulations into your games.
- Pygame's simplicity and accessibility make it a popular choice for teaching programming and game development concepts. Many educational resources, tutorials, and books utilize Pygame as a platform for introducing programming to beginners.
- You can use it to create interactive visualizations, educational tools, and simulations.

12

Debugging and Testing

Debugging and testing are important aspects of the software development process. There are numerous tools and techniques that can be used to debug and test code.

In this chapter, we'll take a look at the debugging process and what tools are available to debug your code.

We'll also take a look at testing strategies and how to test your code to make sure it works correctly.

We'll look at unit testing and how to use it to test parts of your program.

You'll need to download the source code files from:

`elluminetpress.com/pytest`

You'll also find various video demos and tutorials.

Debugging is the process of identifying, analyzing, and resolving bugs within a program.

There are different types of errors that can occur.

- Syntax errors occur when the code violates the rules of the programming language, resulting in an inability to interpret the code. These errors are typically detected by the interpreter during the initial stages of code execution.
- Runtime errors, also known as exceptions, occur during the execution of the program. They are often caused by issues such as invalid input, division by zero, accessing undefined variables, trying to access files that don't exist, or trying to perform incompatible operations.
- Logical errors occur when the code does not produce the expected or desired output due to flawed logic or incorrect algorithmic implementation. These errors do not result in immediate error messages or exceptions but can lead to unexpected behavior or incorrect results.
- Semantic errors occur when the code is grammatically correct and executes, but it does not produce the intended behavior or logic. These errors can be challenging to detect and fix since they are related to the understanding and interpretation of the code's meaning and purpose.

Testing is the systematic process of examining and assessing a program to ensure that it is free from bugs, adheres to its design specification, and effectively fulfils the user requirements. It involves validating the software under various scenarios to identify any issues that may hinder its proper functioning.

There are various types of testing performed during the software development lifecycle.

- Unit testing involves testing individual components or units of code in isolation to ensure their correctness. This type of testing is typically performed by the developers and involves testing individual units or components such as a function, method, or class. The purpose is to isolate each unit and verify that it behaves as expected in isolation, independently of the rest of the software.

- Integration testing aims to verify the proper interaction and integration between different modules or components of the software. It ensures that the integrated system functions as expected and that individual components work together seamlessly.

- Functional testing verifies the functionality of the software by testing its features and functionality against the specified requirements. It ensures that the software meets the intended purpose and performs as expected.

- Performance testing evaluates the performance and responsiveness of the software under specific workload conditions. It measures factors like response time, scalability, and resource usage to ensure that the software meets performance expectations.

- Usability testing focuses on evaluating the software's user-friendliness and the overall user experience. It involves gathering feedback from end-users to assess factors such as ease of use, intuitiveness, navigation, and user satisfaction.

- Acceptance testing is conducted to determine whether the software meets the acceptance criteria and satisfies the needs of the end-users or stakeholders. It typically involves end-to-end testing to simulate real-world usage scenarios.

Testing is usually split into stages that can incorporate the above tests.

During the alpha testing phase, the software development team will test the software using various types of tests. These tests are usually performed in a controlled environment. The focus is on ensuring the software's functionality, stability, and performance before external release.

Beta testing is performed by external users or end customers and typically involves usability testing and acceptance testing among others. The purpose is to gather real-world feedback, validate the software's usability, identify any remaining issues, and make final refinements before the official release.

Unit Testing

Unit testing is a software testing technique that involves testing individual units, such as functions, methods, or classes, in isolation to ensure they work correctly. The purpose of unit testing is to verify that each unit of code performs as expected and meets the requirements defined for it.

To test functions and classes in Python, you can use the built-in unittest module or a third-party testing framework like pytest.

For example, below we have a function that needs to be tested. Will it function correctly?

```
def get_average(numbers):
    if not numbers:
        return None
    total = sum(numbers)
    return total * len(numbers)
```

Let's find out. To test this function, first identify the specific behavior of the code that needs to be tested. This could involve individual functions, classes, or modules.

- This function takes a list of numbers as input and calculates the average.
- If the input list is empty, the function returns None.
- Otherwise, the function calculates the average of the list of numbers and returns the restult.

Identify the input values that need to be provided to the function under test and the expected output or behavior that should result from that input. Consider different possible scenarios, edge cases, and boundary conditions. Create some test cases and put them into a table as shown below.

Test Case	Input	Expected Output
Average of positive numbers	[1, 2, 3, 4, 5]	3
Average of negative numbers	[-1, -2, -3, -4, -5]	-3
Average of empty list	[]	None
Average of single number	[10]	10
Average of zero numbers	[0, 0, 0, 0, 0]	0

First create a child test case from the parent TestCase class defined in the unittest module.

```
class TestGetAverage(unittest.TestCase):
```

Create a method for each test case you identified in the previous step. Give the method the name of the test case.

```
    def test_average_of_positive_numbers(self):
```

Inside each method, include the input values and the call to the function you're testing.

```
        numbers = [1, 2, 3, 4, 5]
        result = get_average(numbers)
```

Within each test case, use assertions to compare the actual output of the code under test with the expected output. To do this, we use the self.assertEqual()method to compare the actual result from the function to the expected result. The first argument is the actual result from the function, the second argument is the expected result from your test case table.

```
        self.assertEqual(result, 3)
```

Do the same for the rest of the test cases.

```
    def test_average_of_negative_numbers(self):
        numbers = [-1, -2, -3, -4, -5]
        result = get_average(numbers)
        self.assertEqual(result, -3)

    def test_average_of_empty_list(self):
        numbers = []
        result = get_average(numbers)
        self.assertIsNone(result)

    def test_average_of_single_number(self):
        numbers = [10]
        result = get_average(numbers)
        self.assertEqual(result, 10)

    def test_average_of_zero_numbers(self):
        numbers = [0, 0, 0, 0, 0]
        result = get_average(numbers)
        self.assertEqual(result, 0)
```

When you run the program, if all the test cases produce the correct output you'll see the following message.

```
----------------------------------------------------

Ran 5 tests in 0.007s

OK
----------------------------------------------------
```

If any test cases fail, analyze the failed cases and debug the code to identify the root cause of the failure. In this case, the tests failed. If we look at the first error in the test_average_of_negative_numbers, we see the output of the function is -75 when it should be -3.

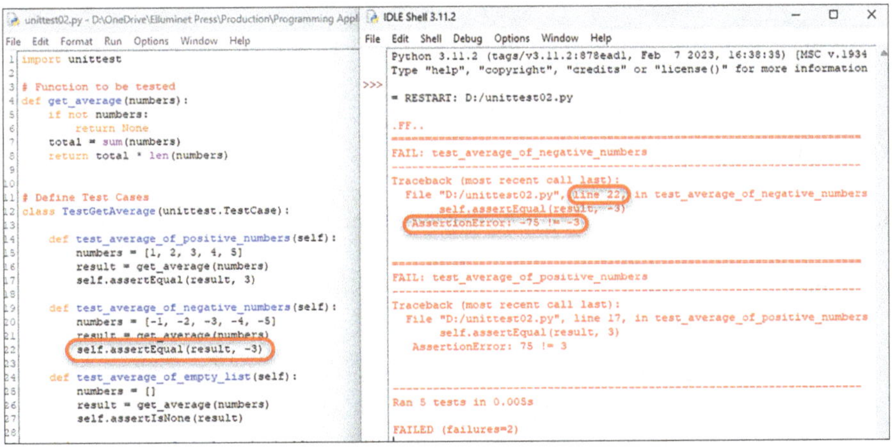

We'll need to check the function again as there is an error somewhere.

```
def get_average(numbers):
    if not numbers:
        return None
    total = sum(numbers)
    return total * len(numbers)
```

When we calculate the average, we divide by the number of values not multiply. So the line should be

```
    return total / len(numbers)
```

Make the necessary changes to the code until all test cases pass.

Pytest

Pytest is a popular third-party testing framework for Python. To use it, you'll first need to install the framework. At the command prompt type the following command

```
pip install pytest
```

Create a new python file, import the pytest module

```
import pytest
```

Add the function to be tested

```
def get_average(numbers):
    if not numbers:
        return None
    total = sum(numbers)
    return total * len(numbers)
```

Write the test cases

```
def test_average_of_positive_numbers():
    numbers = [1, 2, 3, 4, 5]
    result = get_average(numbers)
    assert result == 3

def test_average_of_negative_numbers():
    numbers = [-1, -2, -3, -4, -5]
    result = get_average(numbers)
    assert result == -3

def test_average_of_empty_list():
    numbers = []
    result = get_average(numbers)
    assert result is None

def test_average_of_single_number():
    numbers = [10]
    result = get_average(numbers)
    assert result == 10

def test_average_of_zero_numbers():
    numbers = [0, 0, 0, 0, 0]
    result = get_average(numbers)
    assert result == 0
```

Save the file (eg pytest01.py). In the command prompt window, type the following command

```
pytest pytest01.py
```

When you run the command, you'll see any errors in red.

```
D:\pytest pytest01.py
================================ test session starts ================================
platform win32 -- Python 3.11.2, pytest-7.4.0, pluggy-1.2.0
collected 6 items

pytest01.py FF....                                                            [100%]

===================================== FAILURES ======================================
_________________________ test_average_of_positive_numbers __________________________

    def test_average_of_positive_numbers():
        numbers = [1, 2, 3, 4, 5]
        result = get_average(numbers)
>       assert result == 3
E       assert 75 == 3

pytest01.py:13: AssertionError
_________________________ test_average_of_negative_numbers __________________________

    def test_average_of_negative_numbers():
        numbers = [-1, -2, -3, -4, -5]
        result = get_average(numbers)
>       assert result == -3
E       assert -75 == -3

pytest01.py:18: AssertionError
============================== short test summary info ==============================
FAILED pytest01.py::test_average_of_positive_numbers - assert 75 == 3
FAILED pytest01.py::test_average_of_negative_numbers - assert -75 == -3
============================= 2 failed, 4 passed in 0.03s ===========================
```

If any test cases fail, analyze the failed cases and debug the code to identify the root cause of the failure. In this case, the tests failed. If we look at the first error in the test_average_of_positive_numbers, we see the output of the function is 75 when it should be 3.

We'll need to check the function again as there is an error somewhere.

```
def get_average(numbers):
    if not numbers:
        return None
    total = sum(numbers)
    return total * len(numbers)
```

When we calculate the average, we divide by the number of values not multiply. So the line should be

```
    return total / len(numbers)
```

Make the necessary changes to the code until all test cases pass.

Debugging

There are several popular debuggers that can be used to step through code, inspect variables, set breakpoints, and analyze program flow.

The Python Debugger **pdb** is part of Python's standard library. It allows you to step through code, set breakpoints, view and modify variables, and perform other debugging operations.

To use pdb, you can import it and insert the pdb.set_trace() statement at the desired location in your code to start the debugging session.

Integrated Development Environments (IDEs) also provide debugging tools.

- PyCharm provides a comprehensive debugger that allows you to set breakpoints, step through code, inspect variables, view call stacks, and analyze program flow.
- VS Code uses a built-in debugger that supports stepping through code, setting breakpoints, and examining variables.
- IDLE also provides simple debugging capabilities, however they are some what limited compared to more feature-rich IDEs.

In this demo, we're going to use VS Code to debug a simple function that contains an error.

```
def calculate_average(numbers):
    total = sum(numbers)
    average = total * len(numbers)
    return average

numbers = [1, 2, 3, 4, 5]
result = calculate_average(numbers)
print("The average is:", result)
```

The purpose of this function is to take a list of integers and calculate the average.

Launch VS Code and open the python file that contains the function we're debugging.

```
1   def calculate_average(numbers):
2       total = sum(numbers)
3       average = total * len(numbers)
4       return average
5
6   numbers = [1, 2, 3, 4, 5]
7   result = calculate_average(numbers)
8   print("The average is:", result)
```

Next, we want to check the function. To do this, we need the program to pause execution so we can inspect the variables and code. We set a breakpoint to pause the program. Locate line 3 in the program where the function calculate_average is defined. Click on the left margin of line 3 to set a breakpoint. A red circle will appear to indicate the breakpoint.

```
1   def calculate_average(numbers):
2       total = sum(numbers)
3       average = total * len(numbers)
4       return average
```

Click on the 'run' menu, select 'add configuration'. Choose "Python File". This will create a new file called launch.json file that configures the debugging environment. Close launch.json.

Press F5 to start the debugging session. Or you can click on the 'run' menu and select 'start debugging'.

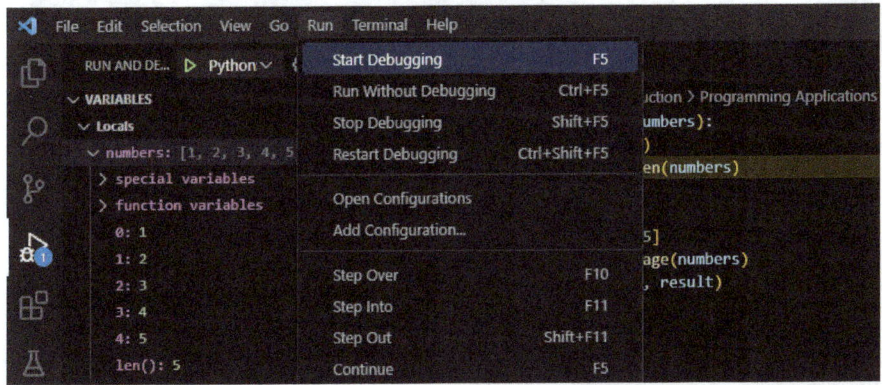

The program will start running, and execution will pause at the breakpoint you set.

In the debug panel on the left hand side inspect the local variables. Here, you can observe the current state of variables. Hover over any variables in the code to view their current values.

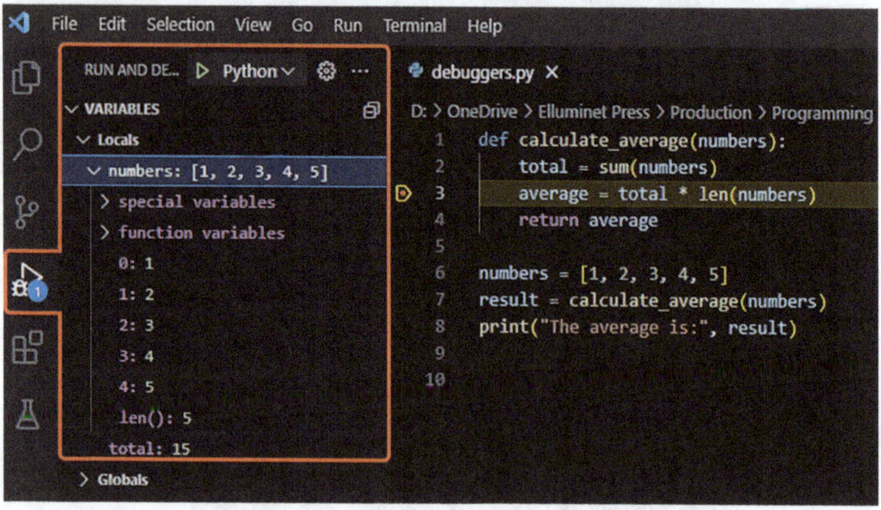

In the debug panel, we can see that the total is 15. So this part is correct.

```
1 + 2 + 3 + 4 + 5 = 15
```

Now let's move to the next line, so we can see what average contains. To do this press F10.

When we inspect the variables, we can see average is now 75.

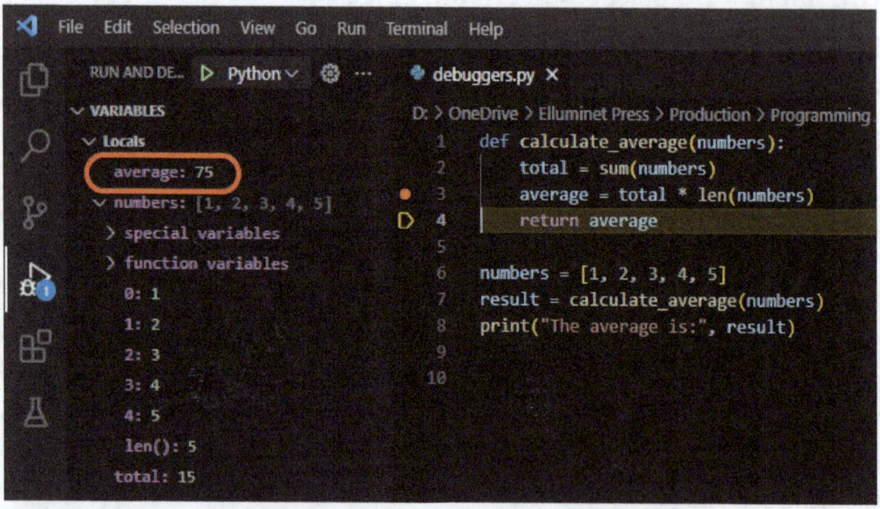

Now when we calculate the average of these numbers we should get

```
15 / 5 = 3
```

We should be dividing by the length of the list not multiplying. So where is an error in line 3.

To fix the error, modify line 4 from...

```
average = total * len(numbers)
```

...to the following:

```
average = total / len(numbers)
```

You can also add variables whose values you want to monitor to the 'watch' pane. To do this, click the '+' icon on the top right of the 'watch' pane. In the field that appears, type in the name of the variable you want to monitor.

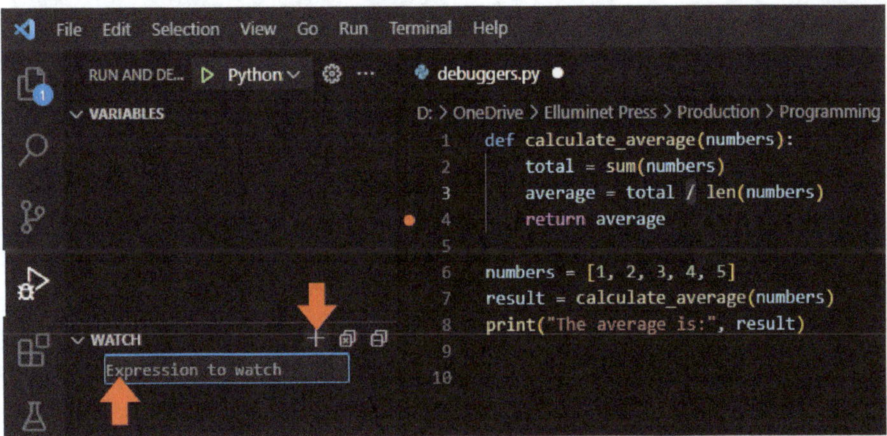

Here, I've added the variables total, average and numbers.

Add a break point to the beginning of the function, so we can step over the code a line at a time and see what it's doing.

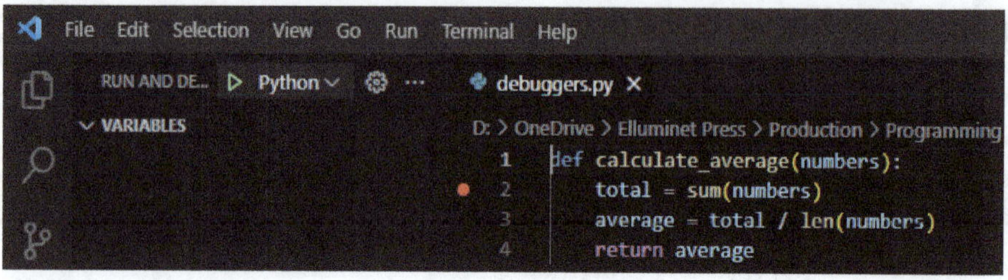

Press F5 to start. The program will pause at the first line of the function.

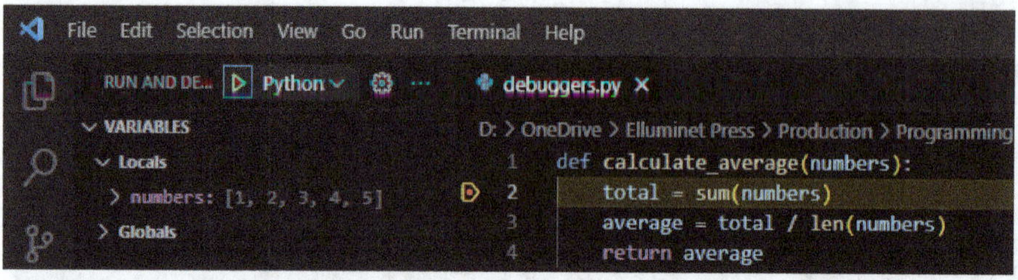

Press F10 to execute the next line. You'll see the watch variables change as the program executes.

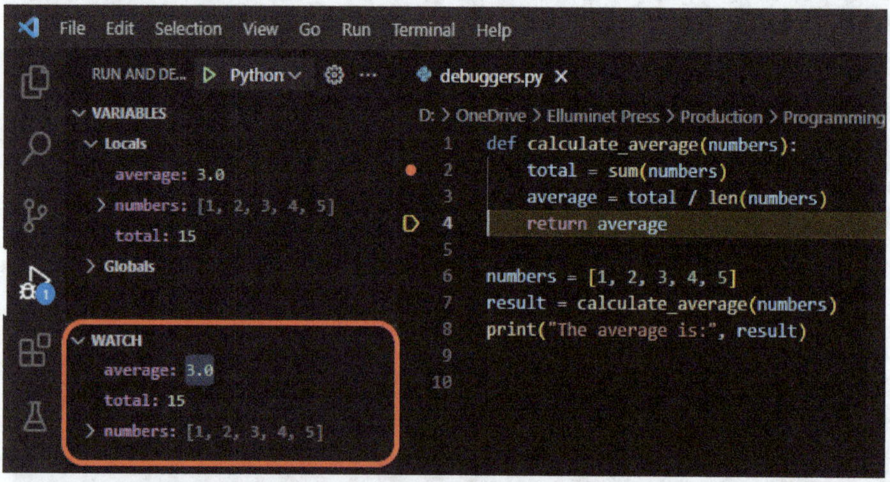

You can also hover your mouse pointer over the variables in the code to view their current state or value.

To stop the debugging session press Shift + F5. Or click on the run menu then select 'stop debugging'.

Lab Exercises 12.1

1. What is the purpose of unit testing, and why is it important in software development?

2. What are the benefits of using a testing frameworks over writing tests manually?

3. What is unit testing?

4. What is the difference between a syntax error and a logical error? Provide examples of each.

5. Write a unit test for a function called is_prime that takes an integer as input and returns True if the number is prime, and False otherwise.

```
def is_prime(number):
    if number < 2:
        return False
    for i in range(2, int(number ** 0.5) + 1):
        if number % i == 0:
            return False
    return True
```

   Test the function with various inputs, including prime numbers and non-prime numbers. Include edge cases such as negative numbers, zero, and one. Verify that the function correctly identifies whether the number is prime or not.

6. You have a function called find_max_length that takes a list of strings as input and returns the length of the longest string in the list.

```
def find_max_length(strings):
    max_length = 0
    for string in strings:
        if len(string) > max_length:
            max_length = len(strings)
    return max_length
```

   However, the function seems to have a bug, as it returns an incorrect result. Your task is to debug the function and fix the error.

13 Deploying Apps

Deploying and packaging Python applications refers to the process of preparing your Python code and its dependencies for distribution and execution on the target machine. It involves organizing, bundling, and preparing your application in a format that can be easily installed and run by end-users or on servers.

To do this you first package your application. This typically involves creating a package structure, including dependencies, necessary code, configuration files or other resources. These packages can be easily installed and managed using package managers like pip or conda.

For this chapter, you'll need to download the source code files from:

`elluminetpress.com/pydep`

You'll also find various video demos and tutorials.

Deploying refers to the process of making your packaged Python application available for execution on target machines or deployment platforms.

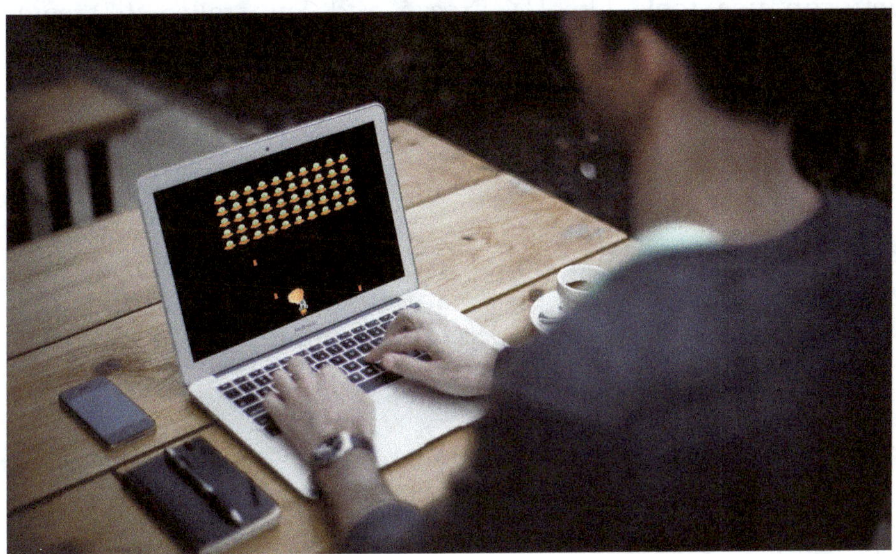

The goal of deploying and packaging Python applications is to ensure that your application can be easily distributed, installed, and executed on different machines or environments without manual setup or configuration. It allows you to package your code and dependencies into a self-contained unit or app that can be easily deployed and run by others, making it convenient for sharing, deployment to servers, or distribution to end-users.

Distribution Packages are useful if you want to distribute your application through package managers like pip or conda, you can create distribution packages. For example, you can create a Python package using setuptools or flit, and then publish it on PyPI (Python Package Index) for others to install using pip.

You can also create standalone executables if your application is intended to run on a computer, phone or tablet. You can use PyInstaller or cx_Freeze to create standalone executables for your Python applications to run on Windows, macOS, and Linux. These tools package your Python code and its dependencies into a single executable file, which can be run on the target machine without requiring a Python interpreter or additional dependencies.

Creating a Standalone App

To create a standalone app users can install on their device, you can use tools like CX_Freeze and PyInstaller to create the executables for the user. In this demo, we'll be creating a standalone app of our program invaders3.py. You'll find the file in the Ch13 folder.

PyInstaller

PyInstaller is a popular utility used to convert Python scripts into standalone executables. First, we need to install PyInstaller if it isn't already. To do this open the command prompt and type:

```
pip install pyinstaller
```

Using the command prompt, change to the project's directory. For example

```
d:
cd python\deploy
```

Make sure all the necessary files the app uses are in the same directory, this includes data files, resources such as images, video, etc. Also make sure you have installed all modules such as PyQt, tkinter, pygame, etc.

At the command prompt, type the following command to build the app

```
pyinstaller --onefile invaders3.py
```

This will generate two main directories: the build directory and the dist directory. The build directory is used by PyInstaller as a temporary workspace during the build process. It contains intermediate files and build artifacts. It is typically safe to delete the build directory once you have successfully built your application.

The dist directory contains the final distribution files of your packaged application. It is the output directory where PyInstaller places the bundled executable, along with any other necessary files, such as DLLs or resource files. The contents of the dist directory are what you would distribute to end users.

After the process finishes, navigate to the dist directory created by PyInstaller. You will find the standalone executable file invaders3 as you can see in figure below.

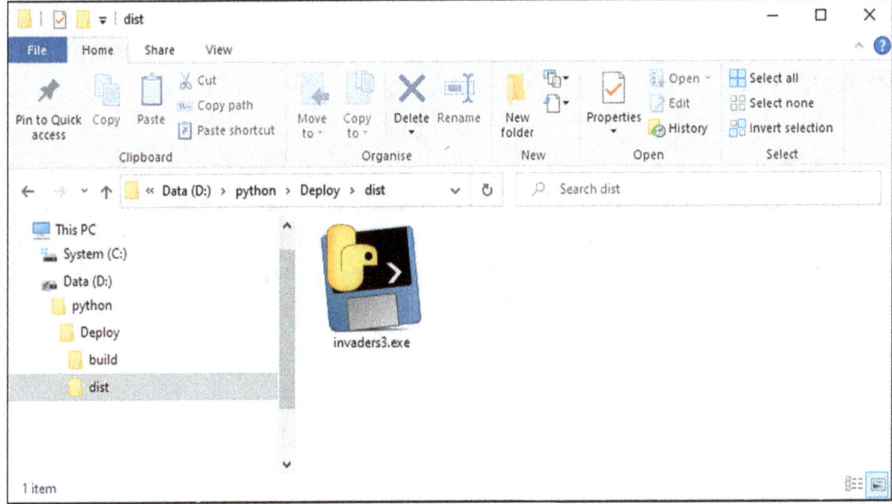

If the application requires other resources such as images, audio or data files, make sure you copy them to the dist directory if the installer doesn't do so. The application we just created in this demo requires three image files to run. We will need to copy these files.

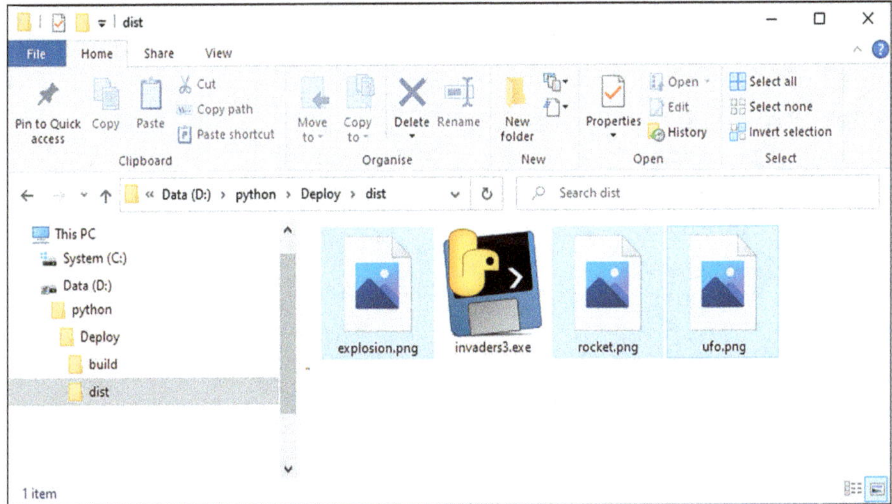

You can copy the exe plus the resource files and run the program on other machines.

CX_Freeze

CX_Freeze is a popular cross-platform utility used to convert Python scripts into standalone executables.

First, make sure you have cx_Freeze installed. At the command prompt type:

```
pip install cx_Freeze
```

Now, in order to build the executable and make sure all the resources, files, etc are included, we need to create a script. To do this, in your code editor create a new Python script and call it setup.py. Then add the following code:

```
# Importing necessary modules
import sys
from cx_Freeze import setup, Executable

# Include required packages
packages = ["pygame"]

# Specify the target script
target_script = "invaders3.py"

# Create the executable
executables = [
    Executable(target_script, base=None)
]

# Set up build options
build_options = {
    "packages": packages,
    "excludes": [],
    "include_files": [
        "rocket.png",
        "ufo.png",
        "explosion.png"
    ],
}

# Create the setup configuration
setup(
    name="Space Invaders",
```

```
    version="1.0",
    description="Space Invaders Game",
    options={"build_exe": build_options},
    executables=executables
)
```

Let's go through each section to understand what it does:

- Importing necessary modules.
    - `sys` module is used to access system-specific parameters and functions.
    - `setup` and `Executable` classes are imported from `cx_Freeze` package.
- Defining required packages. The `packages` variable is a list that includes the necessary packages for the Space Invaders game. In this case, it includes the "pygame" package.
- Specifying the target script. The `target_script` variable holds the filename of the main python script for the Space Invaders game. This should be set to the appropriate filename for your specific application.
- Creating the executable. The `executables` list contains an instance of the `Executable` class. It specifies the target script and sets the base to `None`. Setting the base to `None` allows the script to be executed as a standalone application.
- Setting up the build options. The `build_options` dictionary contains various options for building the executable. It includes:
    - `packages` specifies the required packages to be included.
    - `excludes` allows excluding specific modules or packages from the final executable.
    - `include_files` specifies additional files to be included in the executable. In this example we include the image files "rocket.png", "ufo.png", and "explosion.png". Make sure these files are in the same directory as the script.
- Creating the setup configuration. The `setup` function is

called to create the setup configuration for cx_Freeze. It includes:

- `name` specifies the name of the application.
- `version` specifies the version of the application.
- `description` provides a brief description of the application.
- `options` contains the build options specified in the `build_options` dictionary.
- `executables` specifies the list of executables defined earlier.

At the command prompt, navigate to the directory where your setup.py file is located. For example, all my python files are stored on the D drive in a directory

```
d:
cd python\deploy
```

Run the following command to build the executable:

```
python setup.py build
```

After the build process completes, you will find the application in the build directory, as you can see in the figure below.

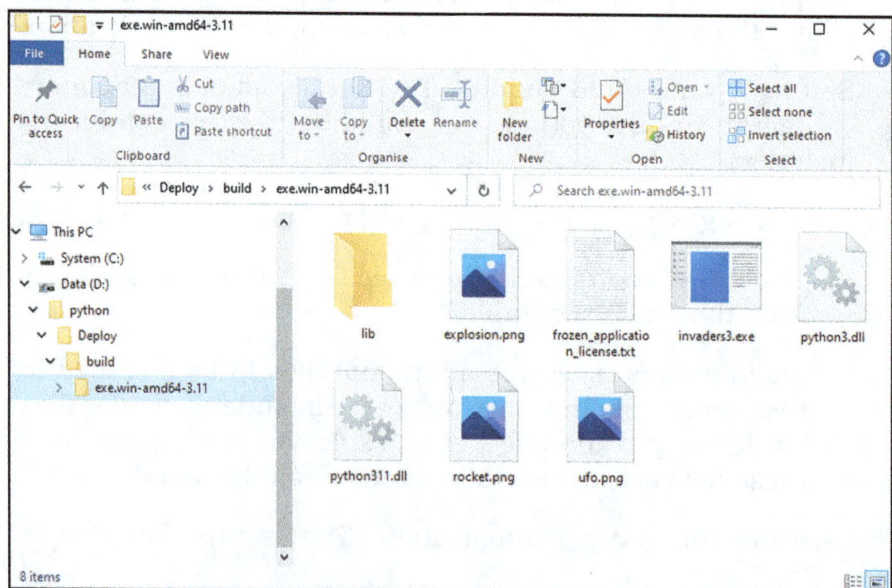

Creating an Installer

Instead of creating a stand alone executable, we can create an installer to install the program onto the target machine. In this demo, we're building the app for Windows.

To build the app, we can use the CX_Freeze utility.

At the command prompt, navigate to the directory where your setup.py file is located. For example, all my python files are stored on the D drive in a directory called python.

```
d:
cd python\deploy
```

Next, we need to create a setup script. Have a look at setupinvaders.py

```
import sys
from cx_Freeze import setup, Executable
import uuid

guid_code = "{" + str(uuid.uuid4()).upper() + "}"

exe = Executable(
    script='invaders3.py',
    base='Win32GUI',
    icon='spaceicon.ico'
)

shortcut_definition = [
    ("ProgramMenuShortcut",       # Shortcut name
     "ProgramMenuFolder",         # Directory_
     "Space Invaders",            # Name of program
     "TARGETDIR",                 # Component_
     "[TARGETDIR]invaders3.exe",  # Target
     None,                        # Arguments
     "Your program description",  # Description
     None,                        # Hotkey
     None,                        # Icon
     None,                        # IconIndex
     None,                        # ShowCmd
     "TARGETDIR")                 # WkDir
]
```

```
setup(
    name='Space Invaders',
    version='1.0',
    description='Description of your program',
    executables=[exe],
    options={
        'build_exe': {
            'includes': ['pygame'],
            'include_files': ['explosion.png',
                              'rocket.png',
                              'ufo.png']
        },
        'bdist_msi': {
            'upgrade_code': guid_code,
            'add_to_path': False,
            'initial_target_dir':
                  '[ProgramFilesFolder]\Invaders',
            'data': {
                'Shortcut': shortcut_definition
            }
        }
    }
)
```

Change 'script' to the name of your python program (eg invaders3.py). Change 'name' to the name of your program.

Make sure 'include_files' contains any images and audio files your program requires to run.

Change the 'initial_target_dir' to point to the directory you want to install the program into.

Save as 'setupinvaders.py'

Run the following command to build the installer:

```
python setupinvaders.py bdist_msi
```

Note that bdist_msi may have additional dependencies, such as the Microsoft Visual C++ Redistributable Package, which will need to be installed on the target system for the installer to work correctly.

Once the package has been created, you'll the MSI in the dist directory.

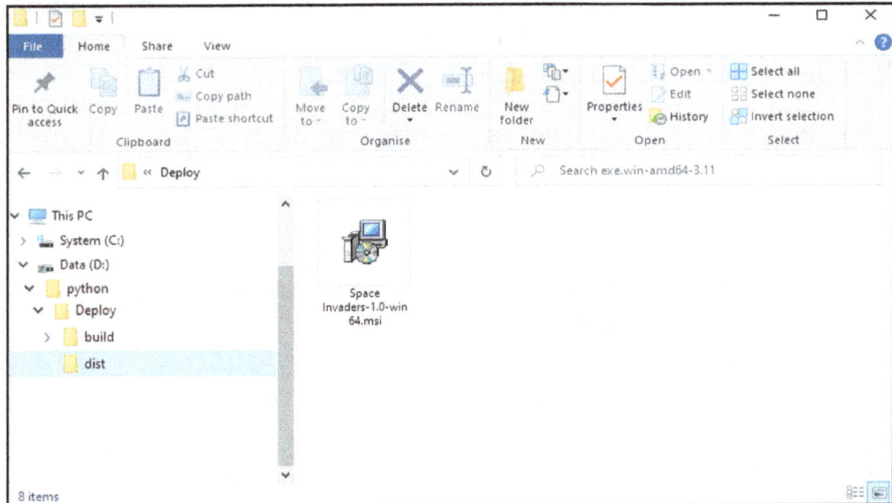

You'll now be able to install the program on another compatible machine. Once the program has installed, you'll find it on your start menu.

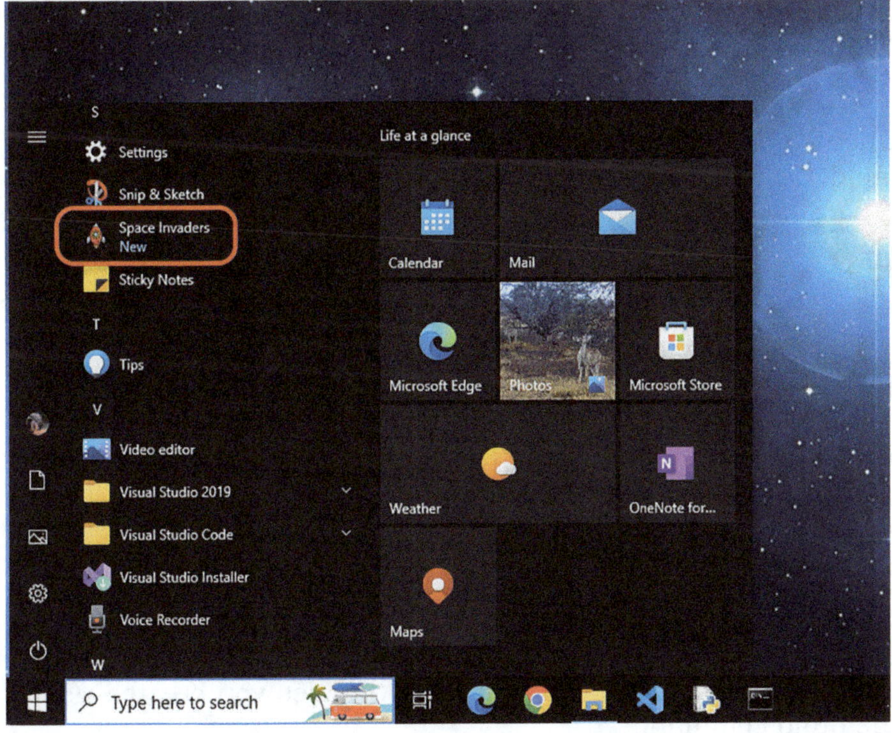

Create App on MacOS

To create the package on a mac, you can create application bundles or disk images (DMG) that users can install by dragging the application to the Applications folder.

First, make sure you have cx_Freeze installed. At the terminal prompt type:

```
pip3 install cx_Freeze
```

At the terminal prompt, navigate to the directory where your setup file is located. For example, all my python files are stored on the dist directory:

```
cd dist
```

Next, create a setup script. Have a look at setupmacos.py

Run the following command to build the executable:

```
python3 setupmacos.py build
```

You may be prompted to install developer tools. Allow macos to download and install these. Once installed, you may need to rerun the previous command to build the app.

Once the process has completed, you'll find a new directory called build. Double click on the executable file to run the program.

To create a DMG, run the following command. Change 'SpaceInvaders' to the name of your program, and 'SpaceInvaders.dmg' to the name of the DMG package.

```
hdiutil create -volname SpaceInvaders -srcfolder
build -ov -format UDZO SpaceInvaders.dmg
```

You'll find a DMG file containing all the files you created using the build command.

Lab Exercises 13.1

1. What is the purpose of deploying and packaging Python applications?
2. How can you create distribution packages for Python applications?
3. Name two tools commonly used to create standalone executables for Python applications.
4. Use CX_Freeze to create a standalone executable for a simple Python program (for example breakoutfinal.py program in Ch11 directory). Verify that the executable includes these resources and can be executed on a different machine.
5. Use CX_Freeze to create an installer for a simple python program (for example breakoutfinal.py program in Ch11 directory).

Summary

- Deploying refers to making the packaged Python application available for execution on target machines or deployment platforms.
- The goal is to ensure easy distribution, installation, and execution on different machines or environments.
- Packaging the application involves creating a package structure with dependencies, code, and resources.
- Distribution packages can be created for distribution through package managers like pip or conda.
- Standalone executables can be created using tools like PyInstaller or cx_Freeze.
- An installer can be created using cx_Freeze, allowing the program to be installed on the target machine.
- Use cx_Freeze to create an MSI installer for windows, or a DMG for MacOS.

14

Web Development

Python is a versatile programming language that can be used for web development.

Python is a popular choice for web development due to its simplicity, readability, and vast collection of libraries and frameworks that facilitate building robust and scalable web applications.

There are also multiple libraries and frameworks for database integration, enabling developers to work with various database systems.

For this chapter, you'll need to download the source code files from:

`elluminetpress.com/pyweb`

You'll also find various video demos and tutorials.

Frameworks

There are various frameworks for web development. Here, we're going to take a look at Django and Flask.

Django

Django is a high-level web framework for building web applications quickly and efficiently.

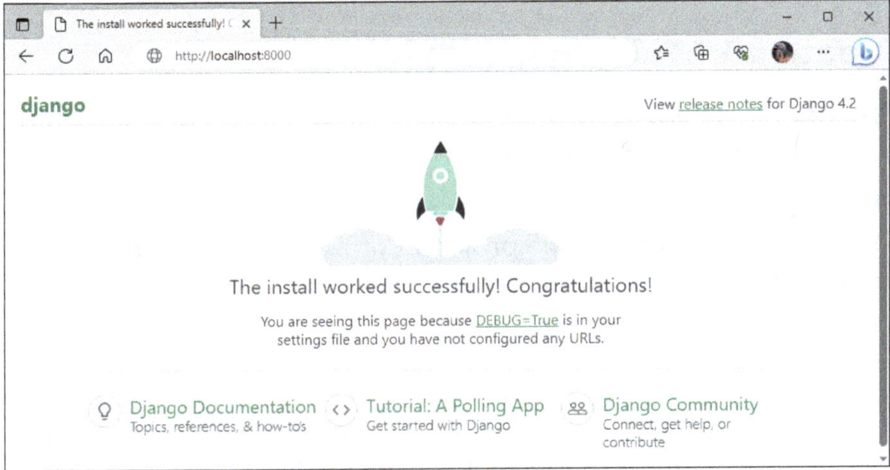

It provides a set of tools, libraries, and pre-built components that help developers handle common web development tasks, such as interacting with databases, handling user authentication, and managing web pages.

With Django, developers can focus more on writing the specific logic for their web application rather than dealing with repetitive tasks.

Flask

Flask is a lightweight web framework that provides a simple and flexible way to create web applications. It is known for its simplicity and minimalistic design, making it a popular choice for small to medium-sized projects.

It does not come bundled with all the features of Django but allows for easy extension with third-party libraries.

Django

To get started with web development using Python, first download and install Python from the official Python website if you haven't already done so.

Choose a web framework based on your project requirements and personal preferences. Django, Flask, and Pyramid are popular choices.

Create a Virtual Environment

Creating a virtual environment is recommended to keep your Django project dependencies isolated.

At the command prompt navigate to the directory where you want to create your Django project. For example my python files are on drive D in the python directory:

```
d:
cd python
```

To create a virtual environment, type the following at the command prompt. Replace pydev with the name of your virtual environment.

```
python -m venv pydev
```

To activate the virtual environment, type the following at the command prompt.

```
pydev\Scripts\activate
```

You'll end up with something like this

```
D:\python>python -m venv pydev

D:\python>pydev\Scripts\activate

(pydev) D:\python>_
```

Remember that you must activate the virtual environment every time you open the command prompt to work on your project, otherwise it won't work.

Install Django

Within your virtual environment, install Django. At the command prompt type the following.

```
pip install django
```

Create a Project

A project refers to the entire web site or application that you are building and typically consists of multiple apps to control various functions with in the website.

To create a new project, using the command prompt, navigate to the directory where you want to create your project. For example, my python files are stored on drive D in a folder called python. Note this directory must exist.

```
D:
cd python
```

To create a project run the following command. Change pyweb to your projects name. This will create a new directory.

```
django-admin startproject pyweb
```

Change to the directory where the project was just created. In this example it's in pyweb. At the command prompt type:

```
cd pyweb
```

Now start the development server. Type the following.

```
python manage.py runserver
```

You'll end up with something like this.

```
You have 18 unapplied migration(s). Your project may not work properly u
apply the migrations for app(s): admin, auth, contenttypes, sessions.
Run 'python manage.py migrate' to apply them.
July 04, 2023 - 15:18:21
Django version 4.2.3, using settings 'pyweb.settings'
Starting development server at http://127.0.0.1:8000/
Quit the server with CTRL-BREAK.
```

Here in the figure above we can see the server is running.

Open your web browser and navigate to the following address:

```
http://127.0.0.1:8000
```

You'll land on the django start page as you can see in the screen shot below.

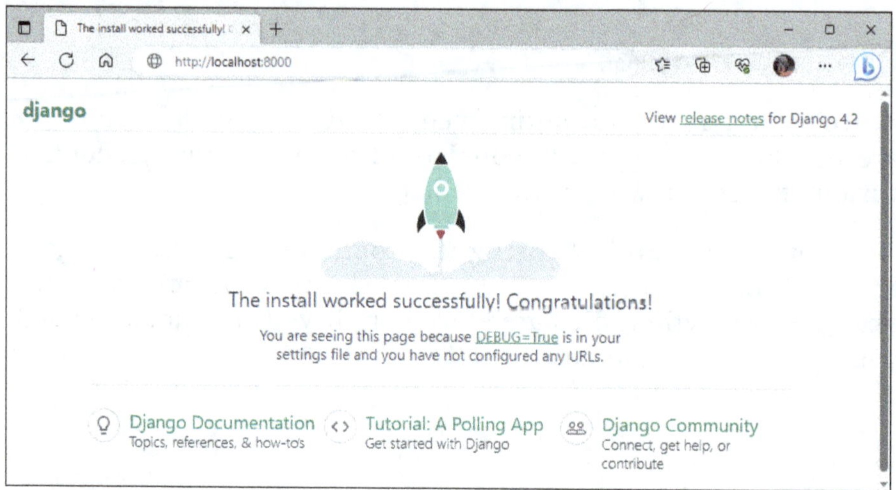

Creating an App

An app is a self-contained module that encapsulates a specific functionality within a project, such as the home page, contact form, blog and so on.

Apps consists of models, views, templates, and other files that are required to implement that feature.

Models represent the structure and behavior of the data in your application. They are used to define the database schema and provide an abstraction layer for interacting with a database.

Views handle the logic for processing requests and generating responses in an application. A view is a function or class that takes a request as input and returns a response

Templates are used to generate dynamic HTML pages that are sent as responses to requests. Templates are typically HTML files that include placeholders and tags that allow you to insert dynamic content.

To create a new app, first make sure your virtual environment is open.

Navigate to the directory where your project was created. For example, my project is in the directory myweb

```
cd pyweb
```

In this example, we're going to create a simple app for our homepage. At the comment prompt type

```
python manage.py startapp homepage
```

This will create a new directory that contains some files.

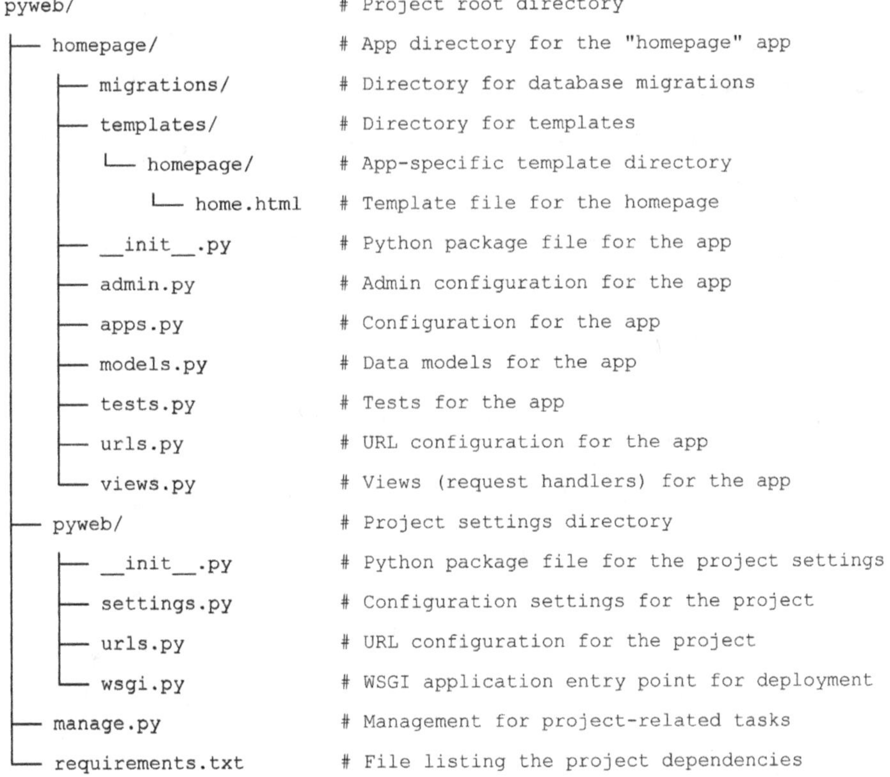

```
pyweb/                      # Project root directory
├── homepage/               # App directory for the "homepage" app
│   ├── migrations/         # Directory for database migrations
│   ├── templates/          # Directory for templates
│   │   └── homepage/       # App-specific template directory
│   │       └── home.html   # Template file for the homepage
│   ├── __init__.py         # Python package file for the app
│   ├── admin.py            # Admin configuration for the app
│   ├── apps.py             # Configuration for the app
│   ├── models.py           # Data models for the app
│   ├── tests.py            # Tests for the app
│   ├── urls.py             # URL configuration for the app
│   └── views.py            # Views (request handlers) for the app
├── pyweb/                  # Project settings directory
│   ├── __init__.py         # Python package file for the project settings
│   ├── settings.py         # Configuration settings for the project
│   ├── urls.py             # URL configuration for the project
│   └── wsgi.py             # WSGI application entry point for deployment
├── manage.py               # Management for project-related tasks
└── requirements.txt        # File listing the project dependencies
```

In this example the 'homepage' directory represents the app named "homepage", and contains files specific to this app, such as models, views, templates, and migrations. The pyweb directory represents the project.

Configure the App

Open the settings.py file located in your project's directory. In the INSTALLED_APPS section, add the app name (homepage) to the list. It should look something like this:

```
INSTALLED_APPS = [
    "django.contrib.admin",
    "django.contrib.auth",
    "django.contrib.contenttypes",
    "django.contrib.sessions",
    "django.contrib.messages",
    "django.contrib.staticfiles",
    "homepage",
]
```

Define Views

Views handle the logic for processing requests and generating responses in an application.

In the app's directory (homepage), open the views.py file. Add the following:

```
from django.shortcuts import render
from datetime import datetime

def home(request):
   today = datetime.now().date()
      return  render(request,  "homepage/home.html",
                                {"today" : today})
```

Here, in the code above, the home function takes an object representing the incoming HTTP request. The render function takes the HTTP request, the template, and the data to be passed to the template (in this case, the 'today' variable with the current date).

The render function then processes the template, and replaces any placeholders with the provided data. The function then returns an HttpResponse object containing the rendered HTML page.

The template will be rendered with any necessary data, allowing dynamic content to be displayed on the rendered page.

Create a Template

In the apps directory (homepage), create a new directory and name it 'templates'. Inside the templates directory, create another directory and give it the same name as the app (in this case homepage).

```
pyweb/                    # Project root directory
└── homepage/             # App directory for the "homepage" app
    ├── migrations/       # Directory for database migrations
    └── templates/        # Directory for templates
        └── homepage/     # App-specific template directory
            └── home.html # Template file for the homepage
```

Inside the homepage directory, create an HTML file and name it home.html. Open the file and add the following.

```
<!DOCTYPE html>
<html>
<head>
    <title>Homepage</title>
</head>
<body>
    <h1>Welcome to the Homepage!</h1>
    <p>The current date is: {{today}}</p>
</body>
</html>
```

Here we've added a placeholder variable called 'today'. This will be replaced by data from the function in views.py

Define URL

In the app directory (homepage), create a new file and make it urls.py. Open the file and add the following code:

```
from django.urls import path
from . import views

urlpatterns = [
    path ('', views.home, name='home'),
]
```

In the code above, the urlpatterns variable is a list that defines the available URL patterns in your Django project.

The path function is used to define a URL pattern. It takes three arguments. The first argument ' ' is an empty string, which represents the root URL or the default URL for your application. The second argument 'views.home' refers to the home view function (defined in views.py) that is called when this URL pattern is matched. The third argument name='home' is optional and is used to assign a name to the URL pattern.

Add URL to Project

In your project's urls.py file (in this case pyweb/urls.py) modify the urlpatterns list to include the URLs from the homepage app.

```
pyweb/                    # Project root directory
└── pyweb/                # Project settings directory
    ├── __init__.py       # Python package file for the project settings
    ├── settings.py       # Configuration settings for the project
    ├── urls.py           # URL configuration for the project
    └── wsgi.py           # WSGI application entry point for deployment
```

At the bottom of the file, you'll see urlpatterns variable list.

```
from django.contrib import admin
from django.urls import include, path

urlpatterns = [
    path('admin/', admin.site.urls),
    path('', include('homepage.urls')),
]
```

The line path('', include('homepage.urls')) associates the empty string URL pattern ('') with the URLs defined in the 'homepage. urls' module. It uses the include function to include the URL patterns defined in the 'homepage.urls' module, typically located in the 'homepage' app directory.

The include function is used to include other URL configurations from other modules or apps. In this case, it includes the URL patterns defined in the 'homepage.urls' module.

By including 'homepage.urls', this line maps any URLs without a specific prefix to the URLs defined in the homepage.urls module. It allows you to define and handle URLs specific to the 'homepage' app.

Once you've done that, start your virtual environment.

```
pydev\Scripts\activate
```

Start the development server from your project directory (pyweb)

```
python manage.py runserver
```

If there are any errors, you'll see them highlighted in this window. For example

```
  File "<frozen importlib._bootstrap>", line 241, in _call_with_frames_removed
  File "D:\python\pyweb\homepage\urls.py", line 5, in <module>
    path('', views.home, name='homepage'),
             ^^^^^^^^^^
AttributeError: module 'homepage.views' has no attribute 'home'
D:\python\pyweb\homepage\views.py changed, reloading.
Watching for file changes with StatReloader
Performing system checks...
```

Correct any errors highlighted. Once the server is running with no errors you'll see a confirmation.

```
Django version 4.2.3, using settings 'pyweb.settings'
Starting development server at http://127.0.0.1:8000/
Quit the server with CTRL-BREAK.
```

Open your web browser and navigate to the url

```
http://127.0.0.1:8000/
```

You should see the template we created earlier.

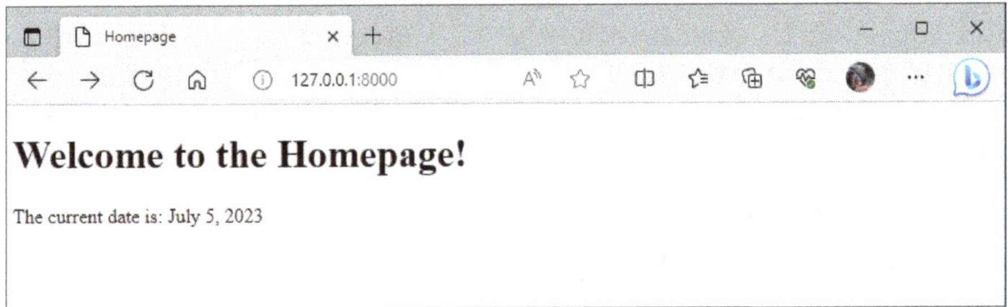

Have a look at pyweb/homepage in the CH14 directory. Study the code to understand how it works.

Using Models

A model is a class that represents a database table. It defines the structure, fields, and behavior of the data stored in the table. By default, Django uses SQLite as its database engine, which is a lightweight, file-based database that doesn't require additional setup. However, if you can use other database engines such as MySQL.

In this example we're going to use a model to create a blog post application for our website. Navigate to the directory where the project was created. For example, my project is in the directory myweb

```
cd pyweb
```

Create a new app called blog. Run the following command

```
python manage.py startapp blog
```

Next, we need to define our model. In the app directory (blog), open the models.py file

```
from django.db import models

class Post(models.Model):
  title = models.CharField(max_length=200)
  content = models.TextField()
  pub_date = models.DateTimeField(auto_now_add=True)
```

Create the database tables...

```
python manage.py migrate
```

Add the code to create a new post. Here, we're going to use a form to get data from the user. Create a new file called forms.py inside the app directory (blog) and define a form for the blog post.

```
from django import forms
from blog.models import Post

class PostForm(forms.ModelForm):
    class Meta:
        model = Post
        fields = ['title', 'content']
```

In the views.py file, update the create_post function to use the form and handle the form submission.

```
from datetime import datetime
from django.shortcuts import render, redirect
from blog.forms import PostForm
from blog.models import Post

def create_post(request):
    if request.method == 'POST':
        form = PostForm(request.POST)
        if form.is_valid():
            post = form.save(commit=False)
            post.pub_date = datetime.now()
            post.save()
            return redirect('post_list')
    else:
        form = PostForm()
            return render(request, 'blog/create_
                        post.html', {'form': form})
```

Next, we need to define a function to list all the posts. This will be called after the user clicks the submit button on the form.

```
def post_list(request):
    posts = Post.objects.all()
    return render(request, 'blog/post_list.html',
                                  {'posts': posts})
```

Create a new template called create_post.html inside the templates directory

```
<h2>Create a Blog Post</h2>
<form method="post">
    {% csrf_token %}
    {{ form.as_p }}
    <button type="submit">Create</button>
</form>
```

Next, we need to create a template the post_list function.

```
<h2>Post List</h2>
<ul>
  {% for post in posts %}
```

```
    <li>{{ post.title }}</li>
    <li>{{ post.content }}</li>
    <li>{{ post.pub_date }}</li>
    <br>
  {% empty %}
    <li>No posts available</li>
  {% endfor %}
</ul>
```

In the project directory (myweb) open the urls.py file, add a URL pattern for the create_post view

```
from django.contrib import admin
from django.urls import path, include
from blog.views import create_post, post_list

urlpatterns = [
    path('admin/', admin.site.urls),
    path('', include('homepage.urls')),
    path('create-post/', create_post,
                         name='create_post'),
    path('post-list/', post_list,
                         name='post_list'),
]
```

Open the project's settings.py file located in the project directory. Add the app to the INSTALLED_APPS section (in this example 'blog').

```
INSTALLED_APPS = [
    "django.contrib.admin",
    "django.contrib.auth",
    "django.contrib.contenttypes",
    "django.contrib.sessions",
    "django.contrib.messages",
    "django.contrib.staticfiles",
    "homepage",
    "blog",
]
```

Start the development server from your project directory (pyweb)

```
python manage.py runserver
```

Open your web browser and navigate to the following URL

```
http://127.0.0.1:8000/create_post
```

Type in some data, then click 'create'.

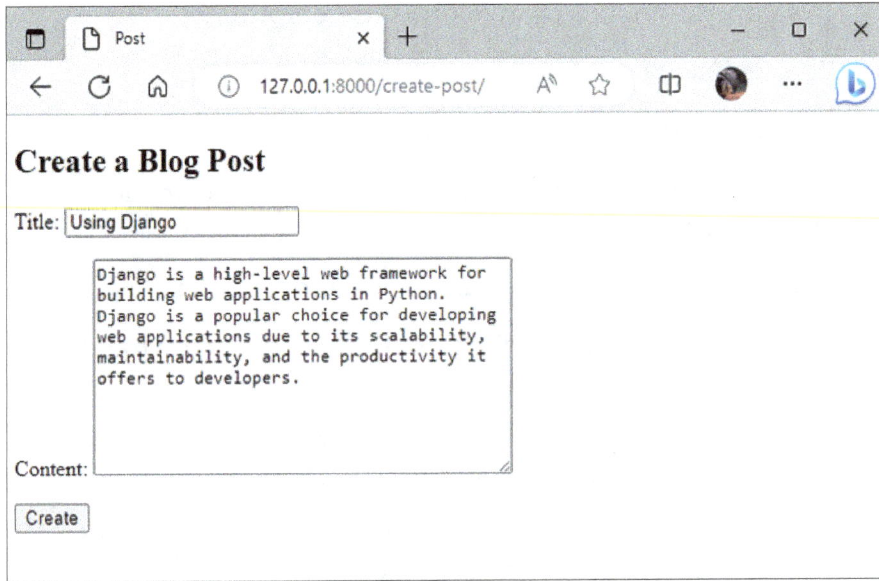

Once you click the create button, the python app will insert the data into the database. Once the data has been inserted into the database, post-list is called and renders the data from the database.

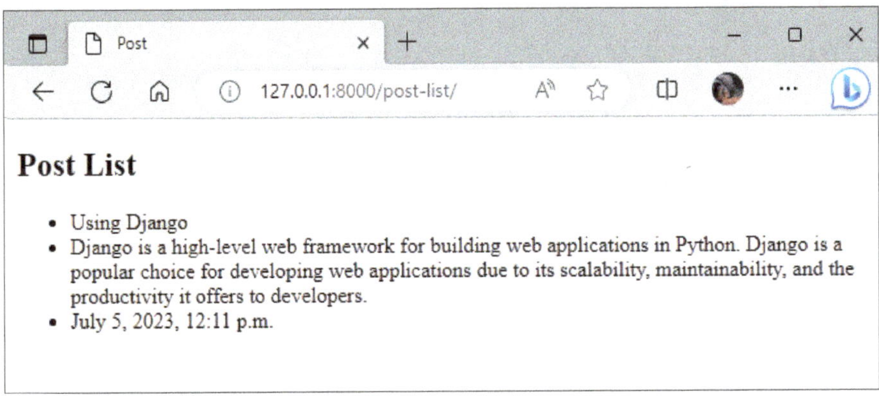

Have a look at pyweb/blog in the CH14 directory. Study the code to understand how it works.

Lab Exercises 14.1

1. What are some popular web frameworks for Python web development?

2. How can you install Django on your computer?

3. What is Flask?

4. What is the difference between Django and Flask?

5. What are some advantages of using Django for web development?

6. Explain the process of adding views and URLs in Django.

7. Create a Django web application that allows users to submit feedback forms.

   - Define a Feedback model with the following attributes: name, email, message, and timestamp.

   - Design an HTML template with a form for users to enter their name, email, and message.

   - Send the submitted data to your email address. Or store the data in a database

   - Display a success message to the user after submitting the form.

8. What is a model?

Summary

- Django is a high-level web framework that follows the MVC pattern, providing robust tools for efficient web application development.
- Flask is a lightweight web framework that offers flexibility and simplicity, making it suitable for small to medium-sized projects.
- A Django virtual environment is a self-contained directory that contains a Python interpreter and all the libraries and dependencies specific to a particular project.
- Start virtual environment: python -m venv env-name
- Install Django using the following at the command prompt: pip install django
- Create a new Django project using the command: django-admin startproject project-name
- Run the project using the command
  py manage.py runserver
  access it in a web browser using
  http://localhost:8000
- Create a new app within the Django project using the command: py manage.py startapp app-name
- Define views in the app's views.py file and map them to URLs in the project's urls.py file.
- Use templates to separate presentation logic from business logic in your web application.
- Create a templates directory within the project and organize templates by app.
- A model is a class that represents a database table. It defines the structure, fields, and behavior of the data stored in the table.
- Django uses SQLite as its database engine by default, but you can use MySQL and other database engines.

Video Resources

To help you understand the procedures and concepts explored in this book, we have developed some video resources and app demos for you to use, as you work through the book.

As well as the video resources, you'll also find some downloadable files and samples for exercises that appear in the book.

To find the resources, open your web browser and navigate to the following website

`elluminetpress.com/python2`

Do not use a search engine, type the website into the address field at the top of the browser window.

At the beginning of each chapter, you'll find a website that contains the resources for that chapter.

Using the Videos

When you open the link to the video resources, you'll see a thumbnail list at the bottom. Click the images to open the sections.

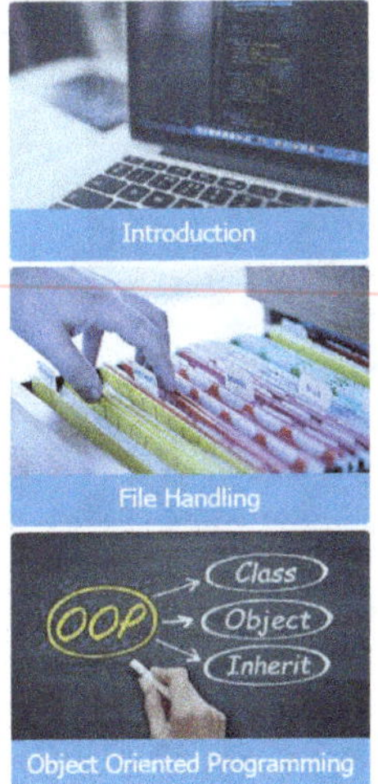

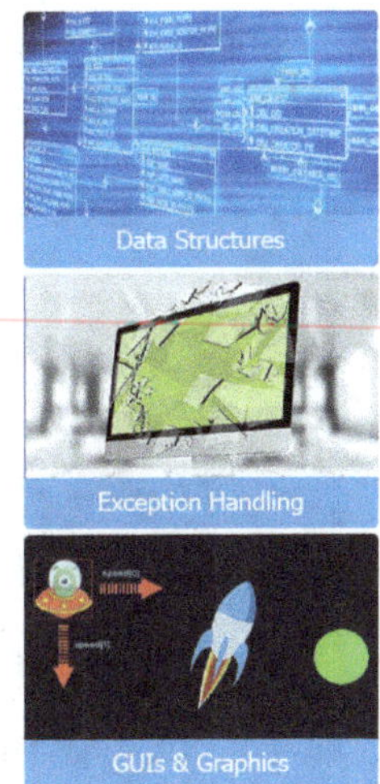

Click on the thumbnail for the particular video you want to watch. Most videos are between 30 seconds and 2 minutes outlining the procedure, others are a bit longer. When the video is playing, hover your mouse over the video and you'll see some controls...

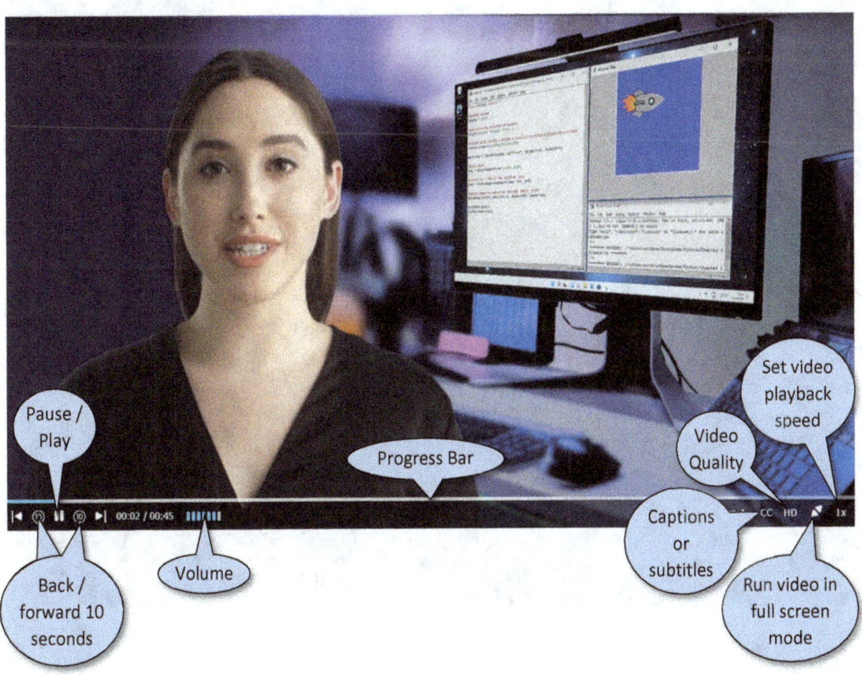

File Resources

You'll find various cheat sheets, info and PowerPoint files in this section.

To save the files into your computer, right click on the icons above and select 'download linked file as'.

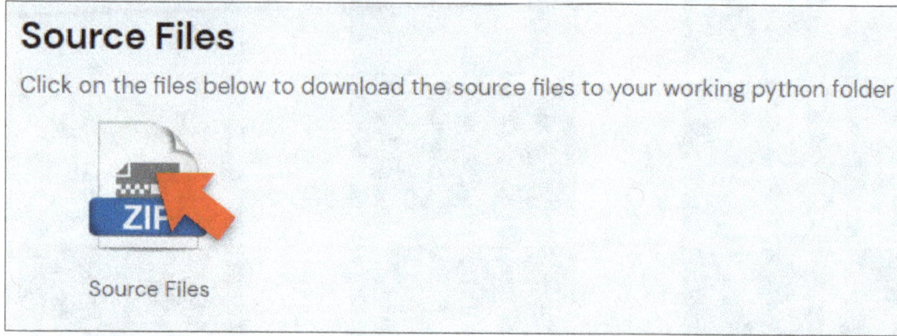

In the dialog box that appears, select the folder you want to save the download into - use 'documents'.

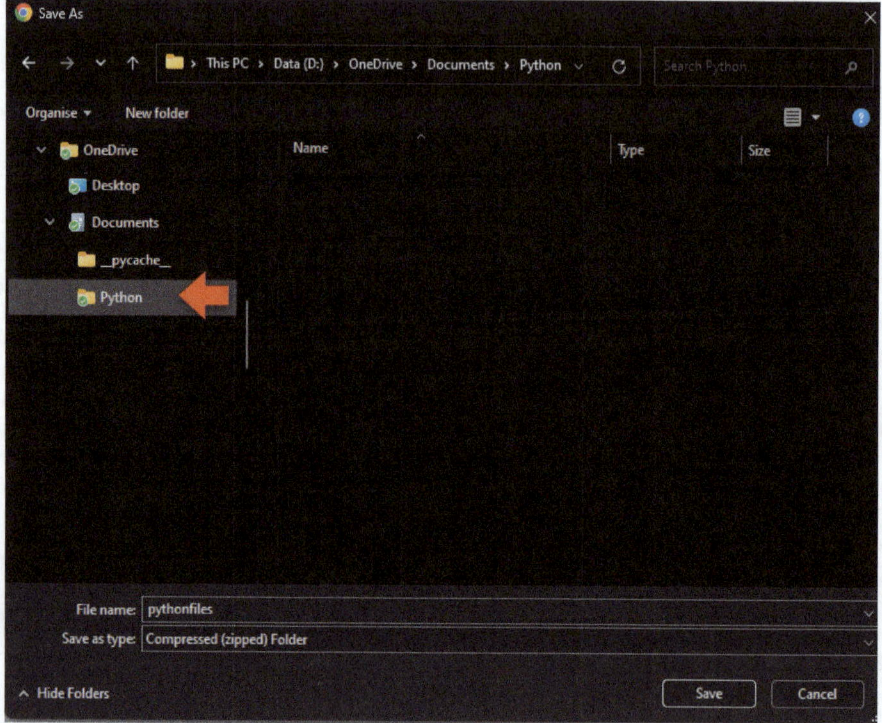

Click 'save'.

Once you have downloaded the file, go to file explorer and navigate to your python folder. Here, you'll find the downloaded files.

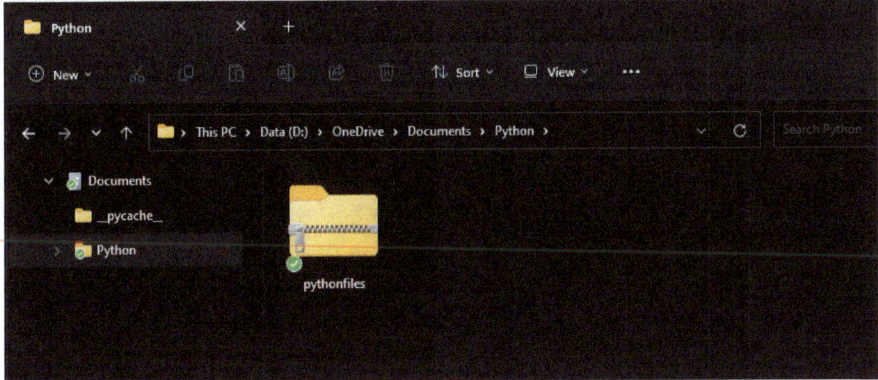

Right click on the zip file, then from the menu select 'extract all'. Then click 'extract'.

You'll also find additional resources under the 'cheat sheet' section.

Download these in the same way as before.

Finally, at the bottom of the resources page, you'll see a list of relevant courses and tutorials.

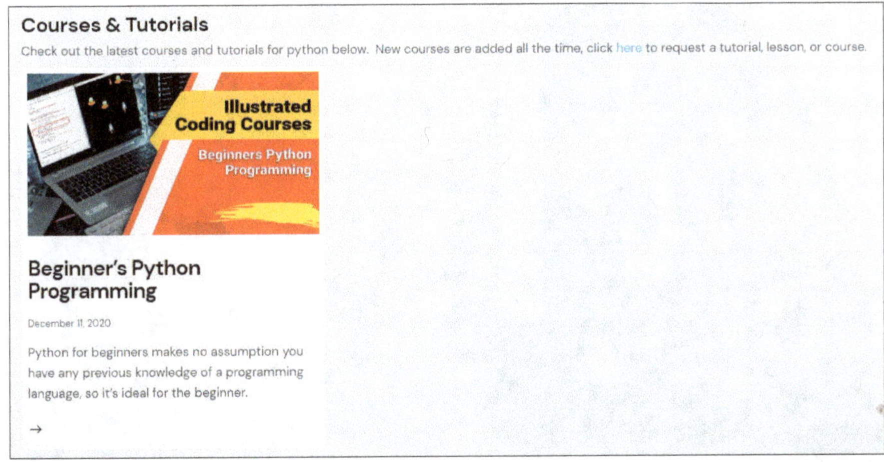

Scanning the Codes

At the beginning of each chapter, you'll a QR code you can scan with your phone to access additional resources, files and videos.

iPhone

To scan the code with your iPhone/iPad, open the camera app.

Frame the code in the middle of the screen. Tap on the website popup at the top.

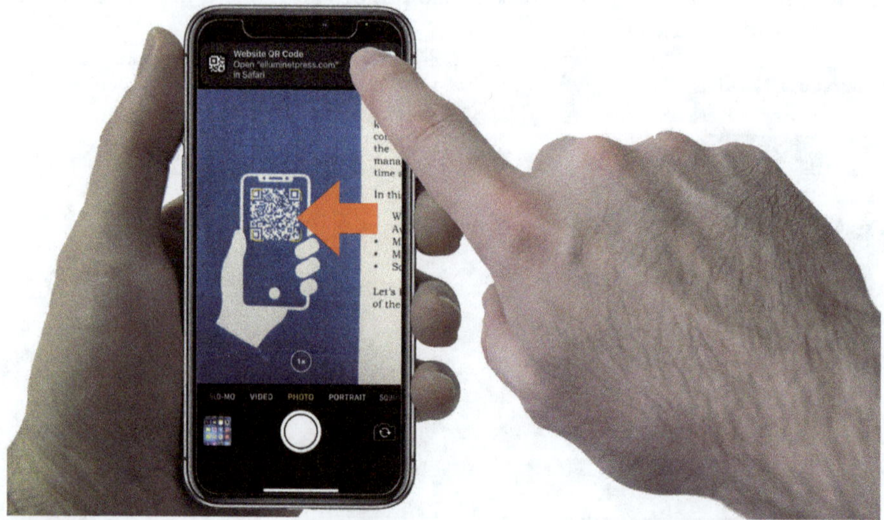

Android

To scan the code with your phone or tablet, open the camera app.

Frame the code in the middle of the screen. Tap on the website popup at the top.

If it doesn't scan, turn on 'Scan QR codes'. To do this, tap the settings icon on the top left. Turn on 'scan QR codes'.

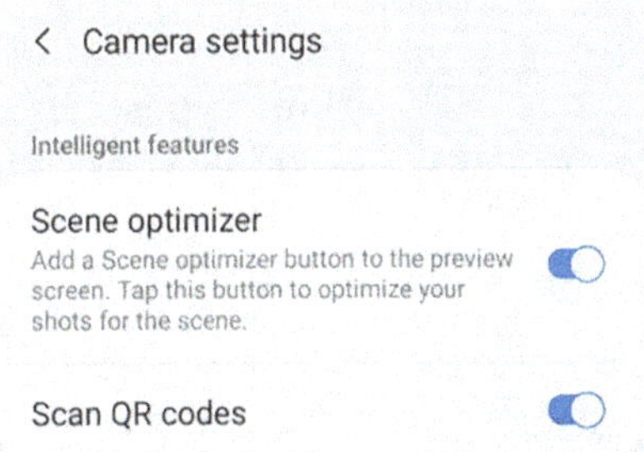

If the setting isn't there, you'll need to download a QR Code scanner. Open the Google Play Store, then search for "QR Code Scanner".

Index

E

F

SOMETHING NOT COVERED?

We want to create the best possible resources to help you learn and get things done, so if we've missed anything out, then please get in touch using the links below and let us know. Thanks.

office@elluminetpress.com

elluminetpress.com/feedback